Winning
THE WAR WITHIN

CHARLES STANLEY

Winning
THE WAR WITHIN

THOMAS NELSON PUBLISHERS
Nashville

Published in Nashville, Tennessee, by Oliver-Nelson Books, a division of Thomas Nelson, Inc.

Formerly titled, *Temptation*.

Scripture quotations are from the New American Standard Bible, © 1960, 1962, 1963, 1968, 1971, 1972, 1973, 1975, 1977 by The Lockman Foundation. Used by permission.

Printed in the United States.

ISBN 0-8407-9036-8

27 28 29 – 04 03 02 01

THIS BOOK IS DEDICATED
TO ALL THOSE WHO KNEW THEY SHOULDN'T
BUT WENT AHEAD ANYWAY.

Contents

DEFINING THE PROBLEM

CHAPTER·1

The Problem at Hand

THE TERM *TEMPTATION* brings to mind different things for each of us. For some, this word conjures up a delicious hot fudge sundae with whipped cream and nuts dripping off the sides. For others, it's the man or woman who has become the focus of secret fantasies at the office. For the businessman who works under unrelenting pressure, it may be the corner bar. For the woman who long ago lost her zeal for being a wife and mother, it may be the corner drugstore where she knows she can get that prescription filled one more time. For the traveling salesman, temptation may mean the R-rated cable movies so readily available in hotels and motels today.

For the teenager, the term *temptation* may bring to mind a can of beer or a pack of cigarettes or a member of the opposite sex who has been declared off-limits by parents. It may be the uncontrollable urge to rid oneself of a meal by forced vomiting, thereby controlling calorie intake. Maybe temptation has something to do with the magazine rack at the local convenience store or the video rental library down the street.

Think for just a moment. When you hear the term *temptation,* what flashes into your mind? What pictures and emotions does it conjure up in your thinking? This is an important question as we begin our study together. In a sense, whatever comes to mind is what this book is all about. It is

11

about you and your particular temptation(s). For some, this book is about drug addiction. For others, this book will seem to speak almost exclusively to the area of sexual temptation. What area of temptation would you like to find covered in this book? What is your greatest temptation?

I want you to choose one temptation or one area of temptation to which you can apply the principles of this book throughout our discussion. As you begin to see God giving you victory in one area, you will be motivated to apply these principles to every area in which you find yourself tempted. But for the purpose of measuring your progress, choose just one area for now.

I've Tried That!

The prospects of overcoming your greatest temptation may seem rather slim to you right now. "I've tried and failed so many times before," you might say. "Why frustrate myself all over again?"

There are several reasons why you must take up the struggle once again. First of all, a defeating habit in your life will rob you of your confidence in the power of God to give people victory over sin. Consequently, you will be hesitant to offer Christ as the answer to others who are controlled by sin. A sinful habit in your life will destroy your incentive to share your faith. You will feel like a hypocrite. And on those occasions when you do muster enough conviction to say something, you will not have the confidence you could have if you were free.

One of the immediate results of being set free from a controlling habit is the desire to share with others the power of God that has been experienced. Satan loves to keep us in bondage to sin because it greatly diminishes our potential for the kingdom of God. It diminishes our potential because we *feel* like hypocrites and we may also *look* like hypocrites if others know about our sin.

I've known several Christians who were never seriously motivated to quit smoking until they committed themselves to making an impact on their world for the Lord. One fellow commented: "Nobody will take me seriously as long as I smoke. People look at me as if to say, 'If God is so powerful, why doesn't He help you quit smoking?'" That's a valid question.

Another reason you must once again take seriously those areas of your life you have allowed to slip is that choosing not to deal with sin ultimately leads to what Scripture calls a hard heart. A hard heart develops when people hear the truth, believe the truth, but refuse to apply the truth. Developing a hard heart is a process that takes time. But each time Christians recognize sin in their lives, feel convicted, and yet do nothing about it, they become less and less sensitive to the promptings of the Holy Spirit. Finally, they reach the point where they feel no conviction at all over particular sins. They become callous, and they quench the Spirit in their lives (1 Thess. 5:19), which is a dangerous thing to do.

The Bible warns that if this process is allowed to continue, God will eventually turn people over to their sin. That is, He will in a sense say, "You want to live your way? Fine, do so, and without any interference from Me." At that point believers lose all moral and ethical direction insofar as the Holy Spirit is concerned. They are on their own. I believe this is what happened to the man described in 1 Corinthians 5 who was carrying on an incestuous relationship with seemingly no remorse whatsoever. I think the man failed to heed the instruction of the Holy Spirit, and Paul said he had been turned over to Satan. Such is the risk one runs if sin is not dealt with.

One Thing Leads to Another

Along these same lines, a third reason you must once again take up the battle against the sinful elements of your lifestyle is that one sin always leads to another. Sin is like a cancer in that it spreads. One undealt-with area opens up other areas as well. Once you become accustomed to a particular sin, once it becomes entrenched in your lifestyle, it is only a matter of time until other areas become problems. It seems like most of the counseling sessions I am involved in begin with a story about some small sin that was allowed to go undealt with. This one area opened the door for other things that soon blossomed into major problems.

I know of a teenage girl whose involvement with soap operas developed an inordinate amount of sexual curiosity in her. After numerous one-night stands and a short marriage that ended in catastrophe, she found her way to our church and told one of our pastors her story. It was unthinkable that someone with her background could ever live the way she found herself living; she was a model teenager at home, church, and school. Yet by her own admission, the afternoon soaps led her into sin that she never imagined possible.

A fine Christian man began stopping at a local bar after work to spend some time with his buddies. He had never had any desire to drink, but he figured one beer wouldn't hurt anything. He even convinced himself that by drinking one beer he would be able to relate to his friends better and maybe get an opportunity to share Christ with them. Before long, one beer became two, then three. Soon he was going home drunk, and eventually he lost his wife and kids. As he told his story to me, he said, "In my heart I knew it was wrong, but I figured every man has his vice." Did he wish he could go back and deal with his drinking problem when it was just one beer every once in a while? You bet he did. But it was too late; the damage had been done.

Sin and Death

One final reason you must take seriously even the smallest of sins is that sin always results in death of some kind. James put it this way:

> But each one is tempted when he is carried away and enticed by his own lust. Then when lust has conceived, it gives birth to sin; *and when sin is accomplished, it brings forth death*. Do not be deceived, my beloved brethren.
> —James 1:14–16, emphasis added

James gives us an equation:

$$\text{Temptation} + \text{Sin} = \text{Death}$$

Whenever there is sin, there is always death of some kind. The most obvious example would be physical death as the result of an alcohol-related automobile accident or suicide. Other sins result in physical death after a prolonged period of time. Examples would include smoking, excessive alcohol or drug consumption, and various eating disorders.

Sin results in death on another level, however, and often the problems on this level lead to destructive habits like the ones cited above. Sin brings death to relationships. Sin causes relationships to deteriorate. When a man is insensitive to his wife, he causes her to withdraw emotionally for a time. If he continues to emotionally abuse his wife in this way, he will eventually destroy every bit of affection she ever had for him. In essence, their relationship will be dead.

If a young couple in the dating stage of the relationship allows physical involvement to take priority over verbal communication, it will be only a matter of time before there is no relationship at all; it will be dead. If an employer neglects his employees, treats them unfairly, and shows no sensitivity to their needs and family responsibilities, in time he will destroy their loyalty to him and his company. If parents neglect children, that relationship will gradually disintegrate until it no longer exists. If a man fills his mind with pornographic material, he will eventually destroy any potential for intimacy between him and his wife. A father who continually ignores the traffic laws with his kids in the car destroys their respect for the law. By example they are taught, "As long as I don't get caught, there is nothing wrong with breaking the law." The teenager who takes just one drink at the prompting of his friends destroys his potential to influence them in the right direction. Sin always results in death of some sort. Something is always destroyed, whether it is respect, loyalty, or life itself.

Excuses, Excuses, Excuses

Think for just a moment. Are you allowing sin to destroy what is most important to you? Are your vices, or "weaknesses" as we sometimes call them, slowly sapping the life out of your relationships with people you love? Do you find yourself lacking the confidence you need to share your faith because of the sin in your life? Have you fallen into the habit of making excuses for sin in your life? Are you ready to allow God to change all that?

Be Realistic!

If you are like many people, you may not have taken temptation any more seriously than you have because somewhere along the way you adopted some erroneous thinking about God's attitude toward temptation. One of the most common statements people make to excuse failure in the area of temptation is this: "I'm just human, and besides, nobody's perfect." Let's take a look at that for just a minute.

There is some truth to this statement. Only God is perfect. The problem is that this statement confuses present character with potential behavior. Let me explain. When people say, "I am not perfect," they are referring to their personhood or character. They are basically saying, "Since I am not perfect internally, don't expect perfect behavior externally." But in a discussion of temptation, character is not really the issue. The issue is whether or not at a given moment in time people (in this case, believers) have the potential to *do the right thing*. God says they do. Paul wrote,

No temptation has overtaken you but such as is common to man; and God is faithful, who will not allow you to be tempted beyond what you are able, but with the temptation will provide the way of escape also, that you may be able to endure it.

—1 Corinthians 10:13

We will look at this passage later in more detail, but suffice it to say that *all* believers have the potential to say no to temptation, regardless of whether or not we are *perfect*. Pointing to character as an excuse for giving in to temptation holds no weight with God. We are all in the process of developing character, but where we are in that process has no bearing on our potential to overcome temptation. It may affect our *desire* to overcome temptation, but not our *ability*.

Are you willing to exercise your potential as a believer and say no to temptation? I hope that you started to read this book because you are willing and you want to know how to proceed.

No Relief in Sight!

Another excuse often voiced in opposition to taking temptation so seriously has to do with the nature of the struggle. It has no end. We will always be tempted, so why should we adopt a lifestyle of continual struggle? Why not just accept certain things as a part of life and not worry about them? The first part of this chapter addresses this excuse to some degree, but this question is important because it brings to light the issues of time and tension. To rephrase the question, since temptation will continue to harass us regardless of how many times we successfully combat it, is it really worth the continual struggle? Absolutely!

Oftentimes we forget that in the process of struggling with sin—in both our victories and our defeats—God is at work. Through the trials of temptation He develops in us patience, endurance, sensitivity to others, and most of all a sense of moment by moment trust in the sufficiency of Christ. On this subject James wrote,

> Consider it all joy, my brethren, when you encounter various trials, knowing that the testing of your faith produces endurance. And let endurance have its perfect result, that you may be perfect, lacking in nothing.
> —James 1:2–4

The apostle Paul understood the value of unrelenting trials in regard to developing dependence on Christ's strength in him. He wrote,

> And He [Christ] has said to me, "My grace is sufficient for you, for power is perfected in weakness." Most gladly, therefore, I will rather boast about my weaknesses, that the power of Christ may dwell in me. Therefore I am well content with weaknesses, with insults, with distresses, with persecutions, with difficulties, for Christ's sake; for when I am weak, then I am strong.
> —2 Corinthians 12:9–10

The awful, never-ending process of combating temptation is God's means of maturing us and conforming us to the image of Christ. To throw our hands up in defeat is to abandon the process and to miss out on life's most important lessons. To grow is to be tempted. We can't have one without the other.

In the mountains of northern Georgia there is a white water river called the Chattooga. People travel from all over the Southeast to paddle down this river. The last two sections are especially treacherous, and many people have drowned as their canoes broke up on the rocks and they were sucked helplessly under by the powerful current. I want you to imagine a skilled paddler in his kayak making his way through the rocks and hydraulics of the Chattooga River. As he maneuvers himself along, something is taking place that onlookers may not be aware of. The potentially destructive force of the river is actually helping the paddler develop his balance, coordination, strength, and concentration.

But imagine that as the paddler approaches the next set of rapids, he thinks to himself, *I'm tired of paddling. This is getting old. My arms hurt. My legs hurt. I'm tired of concentrating.* With that he tosses his paddle into the water and lets the river take control. You can guess what will happen. But here's the point. The force that at one point was aiding in the development of his skill and strength has the potential to destroy him once he refuses to struggle against it.

So it is with the power of sin. As long as we take a stand against temptation, even if we fall momentarily, God will use the struggle to make us into the men and women He wants us to be. But once we throw in the paddle, once we give up and allow the forces of sin to dictate our behavior, it will be only a matter of time until we are swept away and our lives destroyed.

You may be thinking, *That sounds so extreme. My particular problem is not nearly as serious as the ones you must be alluding to.* You may be right. And you are wise to take what seems like a little temptation and deal with it instead of allowing it to take root in your life. But I speak in what may seem like extreme terms because week after week I sit in my office and hear stories of how "little" habits turned into bigger ones. I hear stories of how lives, marriages, businesses, and homes were destroyed because somebody decided that a particular temptation was really not that big a deal and was certainly no cause for alarm. Remember, every *big* habit had a *small* beginning. We don't know the damaging potential of even the smallest sin. And if we wait until things get really bad to deal with them, oftentimes we lose our desire to deal with them at all.

Starting Over

Are you ready to get back on the cutting edge? Are you ready to experience the power of God in your life once again? Then you must be willing to get involved again in the process of working with God to gain consistent victory over temptation. It will not necessarily be easy or instant. There are no magic prayers to say or buttons to push. There is, however, a loving, powerful, heavenly Father who has provided the "way of escape" if you are ready to take advantage of it. It is my prayer that you are ready indeed.

Adult Child of an Alcoholic (or Alcoholic Family)

Anger; Temper Tantrums
Issue of Control,

① Order A.C.A. book That They Show
Buy   recommended

② Celebrate Recovery 12 Step Program
beginning in January 2003?

CHAPTER 2

A Tale of Two Kingdoms

IN THE FIELD of education the "law of integrality" states that learning tends to be more effective when what we learn is related to other areas of our experience. In other words, it is easier to learn something that is clearly related to the world around us than something that seems to exist in isolation from the things touching our lives. I believe that this law kept me from learning geometry. Somehow geometry never related to anything outside the four walls of the classroom. Consequently, my motivation level remained very low—as did my grades!

As we begin a study on temptation, the law of integrality demands that we have a clear understanding of how our individual struggles with temptation relate to the broader scheme of things. It may come as a surprise to you that there is a broader context. When temptation comes, if you are like me, you probably feel very much alone and abandoned. With those feelings comes the feeling that it really doesn't matter what you do anyway; nobody will know, and nobody will care. In fact, what you do always matters. Second, you never struggle alone. Our heavenly Father takes very seriously every victory or defeat in the life of a believer. As we will see in this chapter, every battle, every defeat, and every victory is part of a broader struggle that began long before you or I came on the scene and will continue long after we are gone—should Jesus tarry.

Creation from Chaos

In the beginning God created the heavens and the earth. *And the earth was formless and void, and darkness was over the surface of the deep;* and the Spirit of God was moving over the surface of the waters. Then God said, "Let there be light."

—Genesis 1:1–3, emphasis added

The creation account as we have it in Genesis is a description of God's bringing order out of disorder, creation from chaos. Some people see a time gap between verses 1 and 2 and argue that Satan was cast from heaven during that time, thus bringing the world into a state of chaos. Now I don't want to get involved in that argument here. Regardless of whether or not there was a gap, one thing is for sure. The earth "was" formless, and God gave it form; the world "was" in darkness, and God brought forth light. This pattern follows throughout the creation narrative. He brought order to the water resulting in a separation between the oceans and the sky. He brought order to the oceans and created dry land.

He then brought order to the land by creating plants, each yielding seeds and bearing fruit after its own kind. Then God brought order to the heavens by separating the night from the day. This brought about the seasons and thus a tool for measuring time.

Next God created the different animals. They were perfectly suited for the environment in which they were placed: the fish for the sea, the birds for the air, and the mammals for the land. Like the plants, each brought forth its own kind.

God completed His order by creating man. Unlike the rest of the creation, man had a special role to fulfill. He was to rule over all God had created.

Then God said, "Let Us make man in Our image, according to Our likeness; and let them rule over the fish of the sea and over the birds of the sky and over the cattle and over all the earth, and over every creeping thing that creeps on the earth."

—Genesis 1:26

God told man to

"rule over the fish of the sea and over the birds of the sky and over every living thing that moves on the earth." Then God said, "Behold, I have given you every plant yielding seed that is on the surface of all the earth, and every tree which has fruit yielding seed; it shall be food for you; and to every beast of the earth and to every bird of the sky and to every thing that moves on the earth which has life, I have given every green plant for food"; and it was so.

—Genesis 1:28–30

Man was to be God's representative on the earth. In a sense, God had delegated the responsibility of the whole earth to man; he was to rule over God's creation. This was all a part of God's ordering process.

To ensure that man was equipped for the job, God gave man some special qualities. These are summed up in the declaration: "Then God said, 'Let Us make man *in Our image, according to Our likeness.*'" Much has been written on what it means to be created in God's image. Some things, however, stand out as particularly important when we think about the awesome responsibility of ruling the whole earth. First of all, the image of God implies personality. That is, man, unlike any other part of creation, shares with God an intellect, a will, and emotions. Thus, he has the ability to reason and make decisions—a necessary quality for ruling. This ability also means that man can love, obey, and even disobey.

A Unique Relationship

Second, man's being created in the image of God means that he had a unique relationship with God. Man was and is God's prize creation. Man has the greatest potential of all creation to reflect the nature and character of the Creator. That man was God's favorite is clearly seen in God's special provision for man. God provided a special garden (Gen. 2:8-9). When He saw man was lonely, He created a special counterpart (2:18). He desired man's loyalty and obedience (2:16-17). He desired to communicate with man (3:8). All these things point toward the unique relationship man had with God. It was different from God's relationship with any of His other creations.

Man's Godlike personality and his special relationship with his Creator equipped man to fulfill his role as ruler and representative on the earth. Thus, God's original plan was to rule the earth through man and his helpmate as they exercised their free wills in obedience to and dependence upon Him. This was God's way of maintaining order on the earth.

Back to Chaos

As you know, things did not continue as God had originally planned—humanly speaking that is. Sin entered the world through Adam and Eve, and the whole creation was sent into a tailspin, both morally and physically. You may be wondering at this point what any of this has to do with temptation. The answer to that is found in the answers to some questions you may never have thought about: Why did Satan go to the trouble to tempt Adam and Eve to begin with? What was the point? What did he have to gain?

The prophets Isaiah and Ezekiel give us brief descriptions of a cosmic war that took place sometime before the ordering of the world. According to their accounts, Satan at

one time held a very high position in the kingdom of heaven.
Ezekiel writes of him,

> You were the anointed cherub who covers,
> And I placed you there.
> You were on the holy mountain of God.
> —Ezekiel 28:14

Satan became filled with pride, however, and decided he
should be God. Isaiah writes,

> But you said in your heart,
> "I will ascend to heaven;
> I will raise my throne above the stars of God,
> And I will sit on the mount of assembly
> In the recesses of the north.
> I will ascend above the heights of the clouds;
> I will make myself like the Most High."
> —Isaiah 14:13–14

What ensued was a battle resulting in Satan's being
cast out of heaven along with those angels that chose to side
with him. Ezekiel writes,

> By the abundance of your trade
> You were internally filled with violence,
> And you sinned;
> Therefore I have cast you as profane
> From the mountain of God.
> And I have destroyed you, O covering cherub,
> From the midst of the stones of fire. . . .
> I cast you to the ground.
> —Ezekiel 28:16–17

Satan's rather swift exit from heaven was a sign of ultimate
defeat and humiliation for him. He had been defeated, and

he knew once and for all that a direct attack against almighty God was a futile attempt. Think for a moment. If Satan could not defeat God, what would be the next best thing?

Satan went right to the top of God's order of authority—man. To defeat man would be to defeat all of God's creation on this earth, for it had been put under man's authority. Satan's attack on mankind was simply his way of striking back at God. His intent was to reverse God's process and return the world to a state of disorder and chaos. History is in one sense a record of how successful Satan has been. Man has suffered and so has everything under his authority. God cursed the ground (Gen. 3:17), and since that day, all of creation has suffered. Paul said,

> For the anxious longing of the creation waits eagerly for the revealing of the sons of God. For the creation was subjected to futility, not of its own will, but because of Him who subjected it, in hope that the creation itself also will be set free from its slavery to corruption into the freedom of the glory of the children of God. For we know that the whole creation groans and suffers the pains of childbirth together until now.
> —Romans 8:19–22

The Agent of Decay

Sin is an agent of decay. Once sin is introduced into anything—a relationship, a community, or an individual—order and productivity begin to diminish. The term *decay* means "to pass gradually from a sound or perfect state to one of unsoundness and imperfection." Such is the nature of sin. Satan's goal was to undo what God had done. The introduction of sin or evil accomplished just that. Man's first sin was all it took to begin a chain reaction that sent shock waves throughout creation.

Evil is not a thing; it is a lack in a thing. Evil is a lack of perfection. God's creation was perfect. Thus, He was able to say about it: "And it was good." Evil was and is Satan's tool to chip away at God's order and perfection. Evil reverses everything God set out to accomplish.

The Moral Avalanche

An in-depth historical survey of the worldwide consequences of sin is certainly beyond the scope of this book. What I want you to see, however, is how the introduction of sin caused God's order to crumble. First God's order of authority was broken down. No longer could He trust man to submit to His leadership. Man had made himself a god, and he sought to control his own destiny. Along the same lines, the order of family authority changed. Now the man would rule over the woman (Gen. 3:16). The tone of this verse seems to indicate that such an arrangement was not in God's original plan for men and women. But God knew that sin would result in conflict between men and women, and some provision had to be made to cope with that problem. So He made one the head over the other.

As time has passed, we have seen numerous illustrations of the perpetual slide from order to disorder, from creation, as God meant it, to chaos. Everything from the extinction of certain animals to the abuse of the land and its resources speaks of this downward spiral. The escalation of the occurrence of abortion is another illustration of Satan's attempts to reverse God's plan. Whereas God told Noah and his family to populate the earth (Gen. 9:1), abortionists seek to do just the opposite.

The acceptance of homosexuality and the increasing incidence of people caught up in the homosexual lifestyle are also examples of how Satan is seeking to reverse God's order and return things to a chaotic state. A homosexual lifestyle is the exact opposite of what God prescribed in the Garden of Eden (Gen. 2:24). The feminist movement seeks to reverse the roles of men and women in the home. Now feminists are advocating having children out of wedlock. That way they can fulfill their maternal instincts without sacrificing their independence. One feminist said on the news recently, "Women need to be freed from the constraints of family life while at the same time given the opportunity for mother-hood. Society has held us captive too long with its narrow interpretation of what motherhood is all about." So they find a friend who agrees to make no claim on the baby, and they go to bed together.

Every day the news is filled with illustrations of how the world is seeking to undo all God designed for both society and family. Behind all of this is Satan. In setting this world on a collision course with disaster, he strikes back the best he can at almighty God.

God's Reaction

Fortunately, God has not just been sitting back watching what's been happening. After Adam and Eve ruined things, God decided to wipe everything out and start over.

Then the LORD saw that the wickedness of man was great on the earth, and that every intent of the thoughts of his heart was only evil continually. . . . And the LORD said, "I will blot out man whom I have created from the face of the land, from man to animals to creeping things and to birds of the sky; for I am sorry that I have made them."

—Genesis 6:5–7

But the next verse explains why God did not destroy the whole earth and why He had to come up with another plan.

But Noah found favor in the eyes of the LORD.

—Genesis 6:8

God decided to spare the human race. He was determined, however, not to leave things in the chaotic state they were in. His ultimate goal was to restore man and his world to its original state. But there was still the problem of sin and the curse it brought upon all creation. What resulted was a two-part plan by which sin and its consequences could be dealt with once and for all.

Brand-New People

First of all, God tackled the problem of His relationship with man. Sin had put a barrier between man and God. Until it was removed, the two could never come together as they had in Eden. In sending Christ to die for man's sin, God dealt with the problem of personal sin. Through Christ, men and women have the opportunity to deal with both the penalty and the power of sin in their lives. Before individuals put their trust in Christ, a constant decaying process is taking place; after they trust Christ, a new process goes into effect. The cycle of sin is broken, and a renewing process begins. God reverses the chaotic cycle of sin. Paul was speaking of this reversal when he said,

> Therefore we do not lose heart, but though our outer man is decaying, yet our inner man is being renewed day by day.
>
> —2 Corinthians 4:16

God has re-created us on the inside. We become brand-new creatures when we are saved. Although our physical bodies continue to decay, our inner man—our eternal aspect—is getting stronger and more sensitive to God. That is why we use the term *born again*. This renewal process makes it possible for you and me to rise above our circumstances and live godly lives in the midst of this ungodly society. This inner renewal enables us to overcome even the strongest temptations—as we shall see later on. When we put our trust in Christ, God won a decisive victory over Satan, for He permanently reclaimed us as His own and He restored order to disordered and chaotic lives.

A Brand-New Place

Making men new was only the beginning. Remember that all creation suffered when Adam fell. In order to gain final victory over Satan, God had to redeem nature as well. By nature, I am referring to the physical world. This part of His plan has not been accomplished. The world as we see it today is still in a state of decay. Tornadoes still rip through trailer parks, and people still catch diseases and die. God's victory is not complete until all kinds of evil in the world are vanquished.

In the book of Revelation the apostle John describes what part two of God's plan will be like. The book of Revelation is God's promise to men that He will complete what He has begun in Christ. One day the world will be restored, and evil will be banished completely from the scene. Order will be restored. Creation will be as it was intended to be. John writes,

And I saw a new heaven and a new earth; for the first heaven and the first earth passed away, and there is no longer any sea. And I saw the holy city, new Jerusalem, coming down out of heaven from God, made ready as a bride adorned for her husband. And I heard a loud voice from the throne, saying, "Behold, the tabernacle of God is among men, and He shall dwell among them, and they shall be His people, and God Himself shall be among them, and He shall wipe away every tear from their eyes; and there shall no longer be any death; there shall no longer be any mourning, or crying, or pain; the first things have passed away." And He who sits on the

throne said, "Behold, I am making all things new." And
He said, "Write, for these words are faithful and true."
—Revelation 21:1–5

In the Meantime

By this time you may be thinking that this is really a
Bible survey. Not so! I've taken you through this seemingly
long discussion to make a simple point. A point that serves
as the context for the rest of the book—and the rest of your
life, I might add.

Simply put, the point is that you do not struggle with
temptation in a vacuum. Every temptation you encounter is Satan's way of striking out against God. By attempting to intro-
duce into your life disorder and chaos, Satan continues his
work of undoing all God sought to accomplish in the beginning. On the other hand, every victory you experience is a
testimony to both Satan and the world that God is at work
restoring things to their original state, a state in which Satan
has no place or power.

As a Christian, you are called to be God's delegate to
a lost world. Your message is that God is in the world recon-
ciling men to Himself and that one day He will return to rule
and reign forever. This is the last thing Satan wants anyone
to hear. Therefore, your Christianity sets you up to be a primary candidate for attack. Satan knows that if he can get you
caught up in some sin—however small it may be—you are
sidelined as far as the kingdom of God is concerned. Not
only that, you become a feather in his hat, so to speak. Every
victory Satan has over you is a victory over the advancement
of God's kingdom.

Another reason I felt compelled to begin our discussion of temptation in this way is that it establishes a whole
new perspective on spiritual warfare. I will be the first to
admit that I have a great deal to learn about this somewhat
mystical subject. But one thing I do know is that every temp-

tation is part of a larger struggle. Another thing I know for sure is that I have a difficult time remembering this fact.

When I am being tempted with the little things that pop up every day, I tend to think that it is just my little problem and that no one else will be affected. I forget that I am an ambassador for Christ and that every victory—no matter how small—is a sign to the "spiritual forces" that Jesus is alive and working. Each victory reminds Satan that the same power that gives me victory over sin will one day give our King victory over all His enemies!

Paul could not have been any more clear about this than when he wrote,

> For our struggle is not against flesh and blood, but against the rulers, against the powers, against the world forces of this darkness, against the spiritual forces of wickedness in the heavenly places.
> —Ephesians 6:12

He did not qualify which struggles. He did not distinguish between the big ones and the little ones; the struggles of the mind versus the struggles within relationships; the struggles of the well-knowns versus the struggles of the unknowns. All our struggles are spiritual in nature. Each one is a part of an ongoing struggle between the kingdom of God and the kingdom of Satan. As we begin to look at the specifics of temptation, it is imperative that we keep this simple truth in mind: we do not struggle in a vacuum; every temptation is a small part of a universal struggle between the kingdom of darkness and the kingdom of the living God.

CHAPTER 3

Who's to Blame?

THE OTHER DAY I saw a bumper sticker that read,

LEAD ME NOT INTO TEMPTATION,
I CAN FIND IT MYSELF.

Initially we would all shake our heads in agreement. Temptation seems to be lurking everywhere; we certainly don't have to look for it. Implied in this humorous statement, however, is the idea that we are ultimately responsible for the things with which we are tempted. That is, we don't need any assistance when it comes to being tempted. Interpreting the statement in that light, we may find ourselves thinking twice about its accuracy. We don't like to take complete responsibility for our temptations. It is much easier to blame someone or something else. Yet this tendency keeps many of us from dealing successfully with the besetting sins in our lives.

Alcoholics are classic examples. People with drinking problems have well-rehearsed stories about why they have problems with alcohol. Stories range from family problems to difficulties at work to broken relationships. Regardless of the particulars of the stories, the conclusion is that their problems are really somebody else's fault; if certain people or circumstances would change, then they could straighten up, but not until then. The sad result is that by blaming somebody else for their problems, they never get themselves in a position to change. They short-circuit the whole process.

So What's New?

Passing the buck in regard to temptation is certainly nothing new. It started with the line:

> The woman whom Thou gavest to be with me, she gave me from the tree, and I ate.
>
> —Genesis 3:12

The very first time man was confronted by God about his sin, he blamed it on someone else—his wife! Apparently this tendency ran in the first family because Eve responded the same way when she was confronted:

> The serpent deceived me, and I ate.
>
> —Genesis 3:13

But blaming someone or something else did not work in the beginning, and it will not work now! Even though it was true that the woman did give the fruit to Adam and the serpent did deceive Eve, God held them accountable for their actions and threw them out of the garden.

> Therefore the LORD God sent him out from the garden of Eden, to cultivate the ground from which he was taken. So He drove the man out.
>
> —Genesis 3:23–24

Blaming someone or something else for your particular weaknesses and temptations appears to take the responsibility off your shoulders. But by mentally removing yourself from a position of responsibility, you also remove yourself from a position wherein you could correct the situa-

12/19/02 + 12/20/02

tion. *Until you are willing to take responsibility for your failures, you will be unwilling and therefore unable to do anything about them.* That being the case, if you do not deal with this issue now, the rest of this book—or any book dealing with temptation for that matter—will be a waste of time. In this chapter we will take a close look at what I find to be the most common ways people try to shift the responsibility of temptation.

But That's Just the Way I Am

Many people blame their personality for their inability to deal successfully with particular temptations. They say, "That's just the way I am," or "I've always been this way." I hear this a good deal from men who have a problem controlling their temper: "Ever since I was a kid I've had a hot temper." The implication is that "I have always been this way, and I always will be. There is no use in my trying to change." Often accompanying this way of thinking is a plea to "accept me the way I am."

But the distraught wife and kids have tried accepting him the way he is, and somehow they still find themselves running for cover when Dad gets upset. Accepting him the way he is does not soothe their hurt feelings when they catch the brunt of his caustic language. Not only that, God considers slander, wrath, malice, and abusive speech to be sin (Col. 3:8). God does not excuse his behavior, and no one else should have to, either.

Another unacceptable behavior that often gets excused as part of someone's personality is the habit of closing up and refusing to talk when there is tension or conflict. You may say, "What has that got to do with temptation?" Simply this, becoming noncommunicative under pressure is an inappropriate outward response to one's feelings. It is the same as lying when one *feels* threatened or cursing when one *feels* angry. We don't usually associate closing up with giving in to temptation, but that is exactly what it is. It is a bad habit. And as with many such habits, it is usually defended as part of one's personality: "That's the way I always handle pressure."

Although such behavior may appear to be deeply ingrained into one's personality, it must be changed. I talk to adults all the time who trace the root of their problems back to a parent who would not communicate. The rebellion of a great many teenagers is simply a ploy to gain their father's attention, to force him out of his shell. A noncommunicative parent has the potential to destroy the self-esteem of kids. Therefore, the behavior is a sin and must be corrected. To correct it, however, a person must stop using personality as an excuse.

I'm dealing right now with a teenager who has an extremely difficult time communicating. He has a high IQ and is very talented, both musically and athletically. He and I have concluded that most of his problem stems from his inability to communicate with his dad—the one person he desires most to communicate with. His dad's response to all this is, "I don't like to talk much; that's how I was raised; that's just the way I am." I believe God will eventually deliver this teenager from his difficulty with communication. He will overcome his problem in spite of his father's unwillingness to deal with his own sin. "Sin?" you say. "You mean not communicating is sin?" If it keeps a person from fulfilling a God-given responsibility as a parent or an employee, it certainly is. The great thing is that once someone sees it for what it is and quits excusing it, God can set the individual free!

Can you remember hearing yourself say, "That's just the way I am"? Do you expect people to accept and adjust to your peculiarities? Have you been using your personality as an excuse for the way you are rather than trying to change? If you have, it is time to quit making excuses and begin making progress. To do otherwise is to rob yourself and others of the joy that comes with the freedom of putting bad habits behind you.

It's Everywhere

Another excuse people use is that of circumstances or environment. "If it wasn't for the people I work with, I wouldn't have this problem." "If I didn't have all the pressure at home, I am sure I could change." "It's not my fault. My friends make me do it."

More and more singles are using their singleness as an excuse for engaging in premarital sex. "I'm thirty, and it's not natural for someone my age to be celibate. If I had a spouse, I wouldn't have this problem." And so like many people, they use their circumstances as an excuse. "If only my circumstances were different."

Bart

I was talking to a single man in our church about smoking. For illustration's sake, I'll call him Bart. He believed smoking was a sin. He knew it was ruining his testimony as well as his health. He even quit for a short time. In our conversation he admitted, however, that he had given up hope of ever quitting because all his friends smoke. "I can't quit unless they do," he said, "and I know they aren't about to give it up."

Without really saying it, Bart was blaming his smoking habit on his friends. He put his destiny in their hands insofar as smoking was concerned. In essence he was saying, "Until my surroundings change, don't expect me to change." Granted, smoking carries with it other considerations when it comes to temptation, but Bart never even got far enough to deal with those. He was content to blame his habit on his friends.

You may respond to Bart's situation by saying, "He

just needs some new friends." Though that may be true, Bart needed more than new friends. Like many people, he needed to quit blaming his problems on his associates. Bart's problem wasn't really his friends; it was his unwillingness to take responsibility for his problem. Until a person is willing to do that, he can change friends, jobs, or families and still end up being molded and controlled by his environment.

To put the blame for your habits on your circumstances is to allow someone or something to control your destiny in that particular area. You have handed the direction of your life over to an entity you cannot change and thus cannot control. Certainly, there comes a time to change jobs or friends or whatever is contributing to your problem. But first you must come to grips with the fact that *you* are responsible for your behavior.

All in the Family

A third excuse people are tempted to use is the family. "If you knew the kind of family I grew up in, you would understand why I'm this way." "If you had known my mom, you would know why I act the way I do." "My dad always told me that a real man never . . . and so I cannot . . . to this day."

It seems that I am running into more and more Christians who have been to a counselor or have read books on counseling and now have some understanding of the impact parents make on children and how that can affect them as adults. Consequently, an increasing number of believers have good insight into why they act and react the way they do in given circumstances and relationships. Gaining this insight into the past can be a positive step in correcting problem behavior when it is acted upon. Unfortunately, it seems that some people use this insight as an excuse rather than a tool to aid in the process of change. They shift the responsibility for their sins from themselves to their parents. "If my parents hadn't treated me the way they did, I wouldn't have these problems."

Tina the Talker

Tina was just that sort of girl. She knew as much or more about counseling than I did. When she came to see me, she gave me a detailed description of her childhood; she followed that with an amazing analysis of how her childhood had affected her as an adult. She was able to relate every single thing she was dealing with at that time back to an event or series of events from her childhood and adolescence. I can remember thinking, *We need to hire this girl*. As she talked, I began wondering why she had even made an appointment for counseling. She seemed to understand everything going on inside and around her.

Then I questioned her about what positive steps she had taken to correct her problem. She would evade my questions and explain all over again scenes from her childhood and how they had scarred her as an adult. Soon I realized that Tina did not want help; she just wanted to talk. She had grown somewhat comfortable with her sin. When it really started to bother her, she would find someone to talk to, and that helped to ease the guilt for a time.

I met with Tina several times before explaining to her that her problem was not her parents. It was her unwillingness to take responsibility for her own actions. As I sit here writing tonight, Tina is still bouncing around from counselor to counselor, friend to friend, telling the story she has told so many times—a story that I have discovered is true and could very well be the root of her problems. Yet the story has become an alibi and thus an excuse to allow in Tina's life a habit that will ultimately destroy her.

Let It Go

Having been raised in a family situation that was far from ideal, I know the weaknesses and propensity for sin that can be woven into the fabric of a personality from childhood. I understand the temptation to look to the past as an excuse to allow sin to go undealt with. After what I had been through, it did not seem fair to expect me to change.

But I also know the pain and frustration that such irresponsibility causes to one's family. So there came a time in my own life when I had to leave the past behind and deal with things as they were. It was difficult. Yet it was only after I took responsibility for my actions that I was able to change them. Until that time any effort to improve was only a half-hearted attempt; *really* changing seemed like an unrealistic goal. By the grace of God, however, things did change.

My friend, things can change for you, too. But you must let go of the past. You must be willing to see sin for what it is and then prepare to deal with it. As long as you hold on to your well-rehearsed excuses, things will stay the same. Your parents may have intentionally or unintentionally set you up for the problems you are facing today. However, *you* are the one responsible before God to deal with the things in your life that need to change.

The Devil Made Me Do It

It may have been Flip Wilson who most recently popularized the phrase "the devil made me do it," but this excuse has been around since the beginning. Since we know Satan has something to do with the temptation process, it makes sense that he would be the one to blame. But we need to be aware that the devil cannot *make* us do anything. The Bible says Satan is a deceiver (Gen. 3:13; 2 Cor. 11:3; Rev. 18:23). Jesus called him the "father of lies" (John 8:44). Satan's only power over people is through manipulation and deceit. If he could actually *make* us do things, he wouldn't need to go to all the trouble of deceiving us. When he dangles the right bait in front of us at the right time, we become so tuned in to our fleshly desires that we feel as if something is drawing us toward sin; but it is not a power that literally controls us. In each case we choose to disobey. If Satan could make us sin, the temptation process would be unnecessary.

Think of it this way. Imagine yourself standing at the edge of a cliff that drops off into a deep rocky gorge. Now suppose I walked up to you and said, "We have kidnapped a member of your family. If you refuse to jump, your relative will be brutally beaten and then killed." Have I made you jump? If you believed my story and you believed by jumping you could save your family member, I may have made you *willing* to jump or even *anxious* to jump. But I have not *made* you jump. Even if you jumped and you found out on the way to the bottom that I had lied about the whole thing, I still did not *make* you jump. I simply tricked you into jumping. On the other hand, if I walked up behind you and pushed you off, then I made you do something contrary to what you wanted to do, felt like doing, or even thought about doing.

Now think about the last time you were tempted to sin. Did you suddenly discover that you were sinning or had sinned? Were you in the process before you ever thought about it? Or did it begin with a thought; then a feeling; then maybe a little struggle; then the actual sin? Nobody held Eve down and forced the fruit down her throat; and no one holds you down and forces you to sin, either. Later on we will deal more fully with the devil's role in the temptation process. For now, suffice it to say that he cannot *make* you do anything.

"Lord, How Could You?"

Many believers, some intentionally and some unintentionally, blame God for temptations. In actuality, you are ultimately blaming God when you blame anything or anybody for your weakness in a particular area. God allowed you to be born into your family. He allowed you to meet the group that keeps getting you into trouble. He allowed you to meet that individual you finally became involved with. He knew what kind of personality you would have. If you thought about your sin long enough, you could find a way to pin the blame on God.

But Scripture is clear that God is not the cause of your temptation. James writes,

> Let no one say when he is tempted, "I am being tempted by God"; for God cannot be tempted by evil, and He Himself does not tempt anyone.
>
> —James 1:13

Although James states that God does not tempt anyone, he does not clear up the mystery of why a good God would allow things that lead to our being tempted when He certainly has the power to stop them. This question leads to the whole issue of God and evil. Without getting off onto a completely different discussion, suffice it to say that our good God originally created a perfectly good world. In that perfectly good world were human beings who were given the wonderful gift of choice, and they used that gift as we discussed earlier.

When Adam and Eve made a wrong choice, they made evil a reality. It was always a possibility since they were able to make choices for themselves, but they made it real insofar as human beings are concerned. God is working toward reestablishing a perfect creation once again. In the meantime we live in an imperfect world surrounded by people who continue to abuse the gift of choice. God is not to blame; man is. So each of us is to blame for our own unwillingness and at times inability to withstand temptation.

They Had Every Excuse in the World

The Bible offers two major arguments against our being able to pass the buck in regard to temptation. The first is by illustration. Adam and Eve tried to blame their failures on someone else. Each of them had what appeared to be a legitimate excuse. The serpent really did trick Eve, and Eve really did give the fruit to Adam. How was Eve supposed to know the serpent was lying? She had never heard a lie before. How was Adam supposed to know he could not trust Eve? She had never proved untrustworthy in the past. Besides that, if God had not allowed the serpent to tempt Eve in the first place, she never would have sinned. Maybe it was God's fault after all. Adam seemed to think so. He said, "The woman *whom Thou gavest* to be with me, she gave me from the tree, and I ate" (Gen. 3:12). It's as if he was saying, "God, if You hadn't given me this 'helpmate,' I wouldn't be in this predicament!"

I can remember reading this story and thinking, *Come on, God. Give them one more chance.* I mean, it hardly seems fair that two people who did not know the first thing about deceit or sin or death should be held accountable for such a seemingly small thing. Yet God did hold them accountable, and He threw them out of the garden.

No Place to Run

A second argument for each of us being personally accountable for our inability to resist temptation is found in biblical passages dealing with the judgment. The apostle Paul wrote,

Therefore also we have as our ambition, whether at home or absent, to be pleasing to Him. For we must all appear before the judgment seat of Christ, that each

one may be recompensed for his deeds in the body, according to what he has done, whether good or bad.
                                            —2 Corinthians 5:9–10

According to this passage, Paul's motivation for pleasing God was the knowledge that he would eventually have to stand before Him and give an account of his life. Notice what he said he would have to give an account for: "His *deeds* in the body, according to what he has *done*." Each of us will be "recompensed" or paid back by God for what we *do* in this life. This is not simply a matter of being rewarded for the good things we do. Paul was clear that in the judgment God will give attention to the bad things as well: "According to what he has done, whether *good* or *bad*."

I wouldn't be honest if I told you I completely understand all that Paul was saying in those verses. What is unavoidably clear, however, is that God is going to hold us accountable for what we do—both right and wrong. Paul wasn't counting on being able to excuse his shortcomings because of his tough childhood, his various persecutions, his long nights alone at sea, or his tireless work for God's kingdom. He was expecting to meet God head-on with no place to run and no alibis to try to absolve himself. You and I can expect the same. The Bible makes that very plain.

Who's to Blame?

Have you fallen into the habit of making excuses for the recurring sins in your life? Have you begun to believe your own story so much that you don't feel convicted anymore over sin that used to drive you to your knees in confession and repentance? Have you convinced yourself that God understands your particular situation and surely He will not hold you accountable? Have you found a person or a group of people on whom you can blame your failures?

If you answered yes to any of the above questions,

you must make a decision. The decision you make will determine whether or not you will ever experience consistent victory over sin in your life; it will also determine whether or not you should even finish reading this book. The first step in overcoming temptation is to stop deceiving yourself into thinking that someone or something else is responsible for your actions. God didn't accept Adam and Eve's attempts to shift the blame. He doesn't accept yours, either. Who is to blame for your failure to deal successfully with temptation? You are. To face up to this simple fact is to take a giant step toward overcoming temptation.

CHAPTER 4

The Roots of Evil

ALL OF US have had the frustrating experience of feeling convicted over a particular sin, confessing it, and then turning right around and committing it again. In fact, that may be the very cycle of events that has led you to read this book. Every week people come down the aisle of our church confessing the same sins they have confessed a thousand times. Every summer thousands of teenagers leave church camps all over the country having rededicated their lives in the same areas they rededicated them the previous summer. I know there have been times in my life that I wanted to tell God, "God, if I am destined the rest of my life to fall into temptation, could we at least change the category every once in a while so I will not get completely frustrated?"

To effectively deal with the recurring temptations that plague our lives, we must get to the root of the problem. We find ourselves dealing with the same things again and again because we usually never get to the thing causing us to be so susceptible; we never discover what is setting us up to be tempted the way we are. We deal with sin like my kids used to deal with weeds in the flower bed. Instead of taking the time to pull them up by the roots, they would simply cut them off at ground level. The flower bed looked good for a while, but in a matter of days the weeds were back, making it just as unsightly as before.

The principle we are going to look at in this chapter has the potential to set you free once and for all from things you may have been beset with for years. When I discovered this simple truth, it revolutionized my relationship with my wife and kids. For years I had struggled with something that drove a wedge between my family and me. I would confess it over and over and over, and yet I could not whip this temptation. It was during one of my down times that God, through some friends, revealed this principle to me.

Simply put, whatever we view as our source of security or significance will ultimately determine our actions. Our behavior, for the most part, is determined by the thing or person we believe makes us somebody worth knowing. My son, Andy, rephrased the principle this way, "What we view as our source will determine our course."

For Example

Imagine for a moment two graduate students studying for exams. Student A is not really all that concerned about grades. He believes a person should do his best and trust God with the outcome. Student B, however, has a tendency to equate his worth and potential as a businessman with his grade point average. He knows companies take a student's grades seriously, and because of that, he can't stand the thought of making anything less than an *A*.

That night as they study, they both receive a visitor who somehow managed to get a copy of the exam. Both students are Christians. Both believe cheating is wrong. Which one will have the most difficult time overcoming the temptation to cheat? Do you see how Student B's confusion about his self-worth and security sets him up for this temptation? In the same way many of us have set ourselves up to be tempted. Anytime our sense of self-worth or security becomes attached to something or somebody, we set ourselves up to be controlled by that thing or person.

This principle explains why a businessman who knows he should spend more time at home and less time at work just can't seem to change. Why? As long as his sense of significance and security is wrapped up in his business, he will be controlled by it. This principle explains why a single Christian woman, who knows and believes what the Bible says about being unequally yoked, will turn right around, date, and eventually marry a nonbeliever. Why? Because somewhere in the past she began equating success and fulfillment in life with marriage. Not God's choice of a partner necessarily, just marriage in general.

I see this principle illustrated in the lives of young men in two ways. Some buy into the mind-set that says, "He who has the prettiest girlfriend is the coolest." So they set out to find the "prettiest girl." All the time they know that God's priorities are different, yet they are driven by the desire to be viewed with admiration by their peers. Other guys become convinced that being a great athlete is the way to find significance and an inner sense of security. So they go after it with all their energy and dedication. Soon they begin to live for sports. They know they should be involved at church, but they just don't have enough time. They know they should keep a core of Christian friends, but they would rather be with other athletes. They know they should have daily devotions, but they are always too tired at the end of the day. Before long, football, basketball, or some other sport controls their lives.

I know evangelists whose sense of significance is defined in their minds by the number of people who make decisions at their crusades. Soon that is all they talk about. When things don't go well, they begin to stretch the truth about their results. It isn't that they believe lying is right; they are just too insecure to tell the whole truth.

I have seen couples in our church get so caught up in the social life of Atlanta that soon they are too busy to go to church. Having their kids involved in the "right" clubs becomes more important than attending Sunday school. When they are confronted, they jokingly make excuses and finally say something like, "You're right, pastor. We'll see what we can do." And they usually do nothing. Why? Because what they view as their source of significance and security controls how they spend their time.

A Tragic Illustration

Some of the most tragic examples of how this principle works itself out come from the kids of broken homes. Often a girl who grows up with little or no affection from her father is set up to be tempted to a greater degree sexually than a girl who receives the right kinds of male affection at home. A girl who did not get the love she needed at home may seek it somewhere else. With no conscious decision on her part, male affection may come to mean security to her. The initial feelings she experiences—even in a bad relationship—are so much better than the emptiness she felt before that she gives in over and over again to the sexual invitations of men she knows she should not associate with.

Telling a girl like this that premarital sex is wrong is like cutting off weeds at ground level. It may alter her behavior for a while, but when those feelings of emptiness and insecurity begin to surface again, she will be drawn to get her needs met the way she always has.

Anyone who was brought up in a home where there was a deficiency of parental love will experience a stronger pull toward certain sins than a person who enjoyed a warm, loving home life. The majority of homosexual men who come to our counseling offices are from homes where there was no strong father figure. These men grew up without the male affection everybody needs. Thus, they were vulnerable to the offer of male affection available in a homosexual relationship. As I stated in chapter 3 these unfortunate circumstances in no way relieve people of the guilt or responsibility of their behavior. But if they can understand the connection between their childhood experiences and their present struggles, it is my hope that they will be able to deal with the root of their particular temptations.

As long as men and women seek to gain their sense of significance and self-worth from anything other than God, they will be set up for temptation. Certain people, places, or things will always have an inordinate ability to lure them into sin. Until they change their definition of significance and until they transfer their security to Someone who can give them real security, they will never experience lasting victory in their lives.

Where It All Began

So how did all of this begin? When did man become so insecure that he felt he must attach himself to something or someone else in order to feel successful and worthwhile? Once again we find ourselves looking at the opening chapters of Genesis.

Man, before the Fall, found his significance through his creature/Creator relationship with God. Man was God's representative on the earth (Gen. 1:26–30). By serving and obeying God, man had a reason to live and a great deal of security. It was really a simple system. Man served God, and God took care of man. Man was important because he served and had a close relationship with the God of the universe. What could be more significant than that?

When Satan tempted Adam and Eve, the temptation he offered was really to establish for themselves an identity apart from God. Think about the implication of Satan's words to Eve:

And the serpent said to the woman, "You surely shall not die! For God knows that in the day you eat from it your eyes shall be opened, and you will be like God, knowing good and evil." When the woman saw that the tree was good for food, and that it was a delight to the eyes, and that the tree was desirable to make one wise, she took from its fruit and ate; and she gave also to her husband with her, and he ate.

—Genesis 3:4–6

Satan was in effect saying to Eve, "Eve, God has lied to you. You cannot always trust Him to do what is best for you. You need to begin looking out for yourself. It is time to make some decisions on your own; be your own person. You can be like God. Why serve Him when you can be like Him? Why take care of His stuff when you can have stuff of your own? You don't need Him to take care of you. You can take care of yourself!"

Adam and Eve were tempted to abandon the security and place of significance offered by God. They were tempted to establish an identity of their own apart from Him; and they fell for it. The Scripture says, "When the woman saw . . . that the tree was desirable to make one wise"(3:6). To Eve, the wisdom offered by the tree represented independence. It was wisdom beyond what God had offered. It was wisdom that would allow her to function as God's equal. She would no longer be at His mercy in terms of what she could know. She could know on her own. So she ate.

Paradise Lost

The verse following the exchange between Eve and Satan would be comical if it weren't so tragic. In verses 7 through 13 we find the first decisions of these independent self-made human beings as they strike out on their own for the first time.

Then the eyes of both of them were opened, and they knew that they were naked; and they sewed fig leaves together and made themselves loin coverings.

—Genesis 3:7

The first feeling these "independent, free-thinking" creatures had was shame—certainly not an improvement over
what they had felt under the authority of God. Consequently, the first thing they did was to cover up. They
weren't off to a very good start, were they?

> And they heard the sound of the LORD God walking in
> the garden in the cool of the day, and the man and his
> wife hid themselves from the presence of the LORD
> God among the trees of the garden.
>
> —Genesis 3:8

The next thing our liberated ancestors did was to run and
hide. Now that is no way for individuals who are equal to
God to be acting! What happened to their new sense of security and confidence? Where was all the "wisdom" they were
promised?

> Then the LORD God called to the man, and said to him,
> "Where are you?" And he said, "I heard the sound of
> Thee in the garden, and I was afraid because I was
> naked; so I hid myself." And He said, "Who told you
> that you were naked? Have you eaten from the tree of
> which I commanded you not to eat?"
>
> —Genesis 3:9–11

Adam and Eve's new independence resulted in shame, and
they experienced fear for the first time as well. Fear drove
them to the irrational behavior of attempting to hide from
God. How foolish! But so it is with men and women who
strike out on their own.

> And the man said, "The woman whom Thou gavest to
> be with me, she gave me from the tree, and I ate." Then
> the LORD God said to the woman, "What is this you

have done?" And the woman said, "The serpent deceived me, and I ate."

—Genesis 3:12–13

Now that's a *real* picture of confidence. As soon as God questioned Adam and Eve about their sin, they immediately blamed someone else.

Search for Security

Adam and Eve quickly learned a lesson that takes some people a lifetime to learn. Simply put, man has no significance or security apart from his relationship with God. The creature finds his total value in the context of his relationship with the Creator. Apart from that, there is nothing. As soon as Adam and Eve unplugged (as it were) from God, everything fell apart—both inside and out.

Imagine for a moment that you have been in a terrible traffic accident. When you regain consciousness, you are in the hospital. Soon the doctor walks in and says to you, "Well, we have some good news and some bad news. The bad news is that your arm was severed from your body during the accident." With a great deal of anxiety in your voice you ask, "What's the good news?" He responds, "The good news is that we were able to save your arm." At that point a nurse walks in holding a rectangular box. As she lowers it to eye level, you gasp in horror to find they have saved your arm all right, but they saved it in a box!

In an instant what was supposed to be good news becomes a nightmare. Why? Because your arm is absolutely worthless when it is separated from your body. What was once a great significance to you has become horrible to even look at.

In the same way, apart from a living relationship with the Creator, the creature will experience a sense of purposelessness and worthlessness. There will always be something missing, something that cannot be replaced by possessions, money, or relationships.

Plugged in, But Turned Off

You may be thinking, *But I have a relationship with my Creator. Why do I still find it so hard to resist temptation?* The answer is that Satan is still in the business of deceit. Through his demonic cohorts, he is constantly working to convince us that to really be somebody, to really be secure, we must accomplish certain goals, we must have certain things, we must be seen with certain people, and we must be a part of the "right" organizations. Just as he lured Adam and Eve away from their relationship with God, he lures us away mentally and emotionally so that we look elsewhere for our self-worth and security. We try to meet God-given needs through the ingenuity of our minds rather than the way God intended.

What results is exactly what we saw take place in the Garden of Eden. We live with unnecessary shame. What if someone sees where I live? What if my business associates don't like my car? My son didn't make the first-string football team. I don't have anything new to wear. I didn't make the dean's list. What if people find out what my dad does for a living? I hope nobody asks me where we went on vacation. Like Adam and Eve, we create for ourselves a world of fear. What if I don't have enough? What if my spouse divorces me? What if I don't win? What if I don't get the raise? What if I don't get the loan? What if I have to go to a community college? What if people find out we had to move? What if I lose my job? What if I don't make an *A*? What will happen if I have to sit home this weekend?

Then we hide. We do our best to appear to be something we are not. If necessary, we lie in order to maintain an image. It's not that we think lying is right. It's just something we find ourselves doing to cover for what we feel are our failures or inadequacies.

The Cover-Up

A good friend told me about his battle with lying. Every time someone would ask him about his involvement in athletics as a high-school student, he would say, "I played soccer and ran track." It was true that while he was in high school, he did play the game of soccer as well as run around the track a few times. But he never actually played on the school teams as he led people to believe.

He felt terrible each time he repeated the lie. He would pray and ask God's forgiveness and promise never to lie again. But as soon as he was questioned the next time, he found himself telling the same old story. Finally, one day as he was driving home from a friend's house, the Lord revealed to him the root of his problem.

When he was in the eighth grade, he had tried out for basketball. It was very important to him to make the team. Being an athlete meant instant popularity and lots of attention from the girls. As it turned out, he didn't make the team. The circumstances that led to his being cut were so traumatic that he never again tried out for anything. Although he didn't make the team, his value system remained the same—athletes are cool and deserve attention. This value system stuck with him right through college and into graduate school. Whenever someone asked him about his involvement in athletics, he felt like a failure, so much so that he lied about it.

He was looking to athletic accomplishment to mark him as somebody worth knowing and admiring. In his way of thinking, athletic accomplishments were a sign of a person's worth. Since he had none, he felt compelled to lie. As he described it, it was not really a premeditated sin; he just caught himself doing it. It was an emotional response to a deep feeling of insecurity when the subject of athletics was brought up.

As he was driving home that evening, the truth of his situation dawned on him. Immediately he began renewing his mind to the truth: athletic ability doesn't determine a person's worth. A person's true worth is wrapped up in the creature/Creator relationship with God. That was the end of his lying. He is now free to tell the truth and to laugh at his own inability in the area of athletics.

Making the Switch

Not every temptation you face will be the direct result of a misplaced sense of security and significance. Those that are, however, can be dealt with by simply transferring your value system from the world's standard to God's. By using the term *simply,* I don't mean to imply that it will necessarily be easy. How quickly you are free depends to some extent on how deeply your present value system is entrenched. Perhaps a childhood experience or a series of experiences in your past has set you up for the temptations you have been experiencing. If that is true, you may need a longer period of time to experience total emotional freedom.

Making the switch from your present set of values to God's involves two steps. First of all, you must identify the things and people from which you draw your identity. I call this step of the process *reviewing your life.* It involves answering a series of questions:

1. What do you fear the most?
2. Who has the potential to hurt you?
3. Who hurts you frequently?
4. What areas of your life do you tend to overemphasize?
5. What circumstances make you feel really uncomfortable?
6. In what or whom have you put all your hopes and dreams for the future?

When you prayerfully answer these questions, God will begin showing you the things and/or people around

which you are consciously or subconsciously
security and self-worth. What you are looking
swers to these questions is an *inordinate* amo
dency on any one thing, person, or activity.
are to be admired as well as successful people
There will always be some emotional dependency on a boy-
friend, girlfriend, or spouse. It only becomes negative when
your ultimate sense of security or significance becomes
wrapped up in anything other than your relationship with
God. When your behavior is controlled or at least highly in-
fluenced by forces other than God's standard of behavior,
things have gone too far.

A second step in making this switch involves *renewing your mind to the truth*. To renew your mind, you must
remove the old ways of thinking and replace them with the
truth. We are going to deal with this subject in a later chapter
on a broader basis. But at this point in our discussion the
truth that you need to focus on has to do with the areas of
security and significance. The truth is that all of your security and significance is wrapped up in your relationship with
God through Jesus Christ. Think through these questions:

1. Who created you?
2. Who chose you to live with Him forever?
3. Who holds the power of life in His hands? God!
4. Who is ultimately in control of all that goes on in the
   world today?
5. Who sent His Son to die for you?
6. Who promised He would never leave you?
7. Who promised to be available at any time?
8. Who has the power to bring about in your life all He
   has promised?
9. Who has promised to structure your circumstances so
   that you will be brought to maturity?
10. Who has given you an eternal identity based upon His
    work?

11. With whom, then, does your true security rest? *God/ Jesus*

12. What relationship is the true test of your significance?

My Relationship w/ God Through His Son Jesus Christ

God created you, and He controls when your life on this earth ends. Along with that, His Son has promised to never leave you. That being true, your relationship with God provides you with more security than any other relationship could possibly offer.

In regard to significance and self-worth, God loves you enough to apply His Son's death on the cross to your sins. He accepts you just as you are. What you own, wear, drive, live in, or have in the bank holds no weight with Him. You are significant because He created you.

Begin Now

These are some of the truths on which you must focus if you are to break the power of sin in your life. What you view as your source *will* determine your course. There is no way around this principle. You can confess and promise and rededicate all you want. But until you are willing to transfer your sense of security and significance to your relationship with God, you, like the world, will spend the rest of your life trying to regain what was originally lost in the Garden of Eden. You will be a driven person, always looking for that thing or person to fill a void in your life that your Creator was meant to fill.

Begin today reviewing your life, asking God to show you the things and/or people you have allowed to replace Him. Think through the questions I have listed. Write down the things that come to mind. Then renew your mind to the truth about you and your relationship with God. In time even your emotions will change, and you will experience the freedom God originally meant for you to experience.

CHAPTER 5

The Appeal

ONE OF THE most frightening passages of Scripture to me is found in Ephesians 6:11: "Put on the full armor of God, that you may be able to stand firm against the schemes of the devil." Satan is not haphazardly wandering around tossing temptations here and there. He has a plan, a plan he has tested and perfected. His schemes worked against men like David, Samson, Peter, Abraham, Jacob, and on and on we could go.

This passage is frightening because the implication is that he is out to destroy every believer. That means me, my wife, my daughter, and my son. He is scheming to destroy you as well. If that is true, it is of utmost importance that we understand how he plans to go about doing that so we can be ready to resist him.

Have I Got a Deal for You!

Probably the closest parallel to Satan's strategy to be found in our contemporary society is used by the advertising business. A good advertiser can manipulate your thoughts and emotions from just about any state you could possibly be in right up to the point of believing you must have his product *now!* Think about it. There you are, watching some sort of athletic competition on television. The last thing on your mind is purchasing a new car. Then a car advertisement comes on. The next thing you know, you are sitting there coming up with reasons why it would be advantageous to trade in your old car for a new one! Before you can finish your list, the next advertisement begins, and you find yourself feeling thirsty. Before you can make it to the refrigerator, the next commercial has you dreaming about an exotic vacation. By the time the game resumes, just about every emotion and desire in your body has been stimulated. And you never left the room!

In this chapter we are going to analyze Satan's appeal. Understanding his strategy and learning to recognize his handiwork are important parts of learning to overcome temptation. The temptation process usually begins long before we are aware that anything is going on. Consequently, by the time we catch on to what is happening to us, it is almost too late. I say *almost* because at no point in the temptation process do we lose our ability to say, "No!"

A Paradigm for Temptation

Anytime we try to equate the temptation process with some sort of mathematical formula or series of steps, there will be a tendency to oversimplify the matter. Although I don't wish to paint anything less than a real picture of what is happening, I know from experience that not every temptation falls into a neat, well-defined category. What I am attempting to do in this chapter is to give you the general blueprint Satan uses. Every temptation has its own set of circumstances and actors. There are, however, certain ingredients that appear in every situation. It is these basic ingredients that we are going to discuss.

A good example of what I am saying is found in language study. If you have ever learned a foreign language, you probably learned to conjugate one particular verb as a pattern for all the other verbs. This verb was called a paradigm. As you continued your study, you found that not every verb followed the exact pattern of the original verb. There was enough similarity, though, to aid you in recognizing the form of each new verb. In this chapter we are going to look at a paradigm for temptation.

One Strike Against Us

Another thing we must keep in mind as we study Satan's appeal is that we are not neutral targets. When Adam and Eve sinned in the garden, the whole human race was polluted by their sin. Adam's decision to disobey God and to strike out on his own became interwoven into the fabric of humanity. Everybody is born with a propensity to sin. Theologians call this the "depravity of man."

This is why you do not have to teach your kids to sin. They are able to figure that out all by themselves. This built-in sin mechanism resides in what the Bible calls the "flesh" (Rom. 7:18). When we become believers, the power of sin is broken, but the presence of sin remains. That means that believers do not have to give in to sinful desires, but we will still have those desires from time to time. We will discuss all of this in greater detail later. Suffice it to say, when we are tempted, we already have one strike against us, the presence of sin.

Satan's Aim

Satan's short-range goal in the temptation process is to get us to satisfy God-given needs and desires in ways that are outside the boundaries God has set up. All of our basic desires are ultimately from God. Most of them reflect the image of God in us. For example, the desires for love, acceptance, respect, and success mirror desires we find in God throughout the Scriptures. Only when these are distorted do they become negative characteristics. And so Satan sets out to turn our desire to be loved into lust, our desire to be accepted and respected into pride, and our desire for success into greed.

God gave us other desires and needs in order to demonstrate our dependence on Him and to enhance our relationships with one another. Our need for food and desire for sex are two examples. There is nothing wrong with eating (obviously). But here again, Satan takes this natural, God-given need and distorts it. As a result, some people destroy their bodies by overeating or eating the wrong things; others starve themselves for fear of being overweight.

Of all the gifts God gave humanity, sex is probably the one Satan distorts and abuses the most. Sex was given to mankind to make possible a unique relationship between a man and a woman. The desire is from God. The philosophy concerning sex today is from Satan. God says, "One man for one woman for life." Satan says, "Any man for any woman until you are ready for someone else." God says, "Sex is to be a part of the marriage relationship." Satan says, "Sex *is* the relationship." God is not against sex any more than He is against food, love, or success. But He is against the gratification of that desire, or any desire, outside the confines He has lovingly and skillfully designed.

"The Things in the World"

The apostle John in his first epistle grouped all of Satan's distortions into three categories. He wrote,

> Do not love the world, nor the things in the world. If anyone loves the world, the love of the Father is not in him. For all that is in the world, the *lust of the flesh* and the *lust of the eyes* and the *boastful pride of life*, is not from the Father, but is from the world.
> —1 John 2:15–16, emphasis added

Every single time we are tempted, we are tempted through one of those three avenues. The lust of the flesh represents our appetites, our cravings, our desires, and our hungers. The lust of the eyes includes those things we see that spark our different desires and appetites. The boastful pride of life refers to anything that promotes or elevates a sense of independence from God—anything that causes us to think we can do our own thing, live our own kind of life, have it our way. In all three cases we can see how these are simply distortions of some of God's most precious gifts to us.

Now let's go back to Genesis 3 and watch how Satan used those three avenues to deceive Eve. Keep in mind that we are looking for Satan's strategy: the methods he uses to get people to meet their God-given needs in ways that are outside the boundaries God has set up.

The Temptation of Eve

The account of Eve's temptation begins with Satan causing Eve to doubt God (Gen. 3:1–4). Oftentimes this is a major part of the temptation process. For now, however, I want to skip over this particular aspect of temptation and get right to Satan's attempt to distort Eve's God-given needs and desires.

> And the serpent said to the woman, "You surely shall not die! For God knows that in the day you eat from it your eyes will be opened, and you will be like God, knowing good and evil." When the woman saw that the tree was good for food, and that it was a delight to the eyes, and that the tree was desirable to make one wise, she took from its fruit and ate.
>
> —Genesis 3:4–6

First Satan chose to appeal to Eve's pride. Notice his first offer: " . . . your eyes will be opened." Satan offered insight, knowledge, and understanding. "Certainly there cannot be anything wrong with any of those things," Eve may have said to herself. "Why, the Lord God is always teaching us new things. How could He blame us for wanting to find out a few things on our own?"

Next Satan offered power and authority: ". . . and you will be like God." "Well, there is certainly nothing wrong with this," Eve could have rationalized. "God wants us to have authority. He put this whole garden under our care." Once again she would have been right. But once again Satan was pushing a God-given desire beyond God's parameters.

There was nothing wrong with wanting to increase in knowledge and understanding. That very desire has driven engineers and scientists for decades. Man's insatiable curiosity and desire for knowledge brought about the computer I use to write as well as the paper upon which this book is printed. In the same vein, there was nothing wrong with Eve's desire for authority and power. That, too, is God-given. This is clear because God promises both as rewards to those who are faithful to Him in this life (Matt. 20:23–28; Rev. 20:4). But when these are exercised apart from God's direction, they become destructive and unjust.

"Good for Food"

After appealing to Eve through her pride, Satan used her appetite, her "lust of the flesh" as John put it: "The woman saw that the tree was good for *food*." Once again we can hear Eve arguing, "Well, if God didn't really want me to eat it, He shouldn't have made it edible! Why give me an appetite for food and then create food I can't eat?" Sounds pretty good to me. And it must have sounded pretty good to her.

Next he used the "lust of the eyes": "The woman saw that the tree was good for food, and that it was a *delight to the eyes*." We don't really know what kind of fruit it was. We usually think of an apple when we hear this story. But that is purely conjecture. Whatever it was it must have been unique to this particular tree and extremely appetizing to look at. The very sight of it made Eve want to eat.

We may be tempted to ask, "Is that a sin? Didn't God put in Eve's body the mechanisms to send a 'pick it and eat' signal to her brain when she saw appetizing food?" Of course He did. We have all seen food or even pictures of food that made us feel hungry. There is nothing wrong with that. The problem was not Eve's appetite; it was the manner in which she chose to satisfy her appetite.

"But Why Would I Feel This Way If God . . ."

It seems like every week someone comes into my office with a story that ends, "If God doesn't want me to _____, then why do I feel the way I do?" or "Why would God give me such a strong desire to _____ if He didn't want me to fulfill it?" These arguments sound convincing. Think about it. What kind of God gives His creatures desires they are not allowed to fulfill? But these people are asking the wrong questions. It is not, "*Why* won't God let me fulfill my desires?" It should be, "*When* in God's perfect timing can I fulfill my desires?" Or "*How* would God prefer me to fulfill my desires?"

A couple came into my office several years ago for premarital counseling. As we began talking, I got the impression there was something they were not telling me. I turned to the young man and said, "Have the two of you been sleeping together?" He glanced quickly at her and then back at me. That told me all I needed to know. Before he could answer, his bride-to-be blurted out, "We love each other."

As we continued to talk, they both defended their actions by explaining how strong their attraction was for each other. "God understands. He allowed us to feel this way." Then I asked a question that left them both speechless. I turned to the young man and said, "What are you going to do when you meet a woman at work to whom you feel a strong physical attraction? Are you going to use the same rationale? 'If God didn't want me to meet this need, He wouldn't have let me feel this way?'"

We forget that although God gave us the potential to feel and desire certain things, Satan has the ability to manipulate and misdirect those feelings and desires. That is the essence of temptation. Satan's appeal to you and me is to meet God-given needs and fulfill God-given desires the easiest, quickest, and least painful way.

Taking the Easy Way Out

An old friend of mine burst into my office one afternoon and said, "Charles, I've got to talk to you." I told my secretary to hold my calls, pushed what I was working on out of the way, and began to listen. He said, "Pastor, you know my business has been rocking along at a steady pace of growth. Nothing to write home about, but it is growing slowly." Jim had started his own printing company a few years back. Actually he had done quite well. He had been a faithful contributor to the church and to other ministries as well.

"Well, last week a man came by to see me and offered to buy me out. He offered me almost twice what my business is worth. If I sell, he will keep me on as president and increase my pay. That means I can stay in the work I love without the headaches of owning my own business."

"What's the problem?" I asked.

"If I sell out," he said, "I won't have total control over what is printed anymore. Not only that, I will not be able to give off the gross income of the business. In fact, my giving will be cut to a percentage of my personal salary."

As we talked, I began to see Jim's struggle a little clearer. As it would for most men, the lure of more money had a strong appeal. That along with the prospects of less pressure and responsibility made it seem ridiculous to think about turning down the man's offer. Besides, there is nothing wrong with making more money; and there is certainly nothing wrong with easing the pressure at work.

As we talked, however, Jim realized that what he would give up by selling his company was far greater than what he would gain. He knew in his heart that God led him to start his company and that God had guided him every step of the way. "This would be the easy thing to do," he said, "but not the right thing." He was convinced that he needed to do something about the pressure he was under. But this was not God's plan for meeting that need. He decided to keep his company and wait for God to provide another solution to the pressure problem.

In the following months Jim was able to restructure his company so that almost all the day-to-day pressure was shifted to his employees. He began to enjoy what he was doing more than ever. Since that time, his business has almost doubled.

It's Really All the Same

Whether it is a long, drawn-out situation like Jim's or simply an opportunity to walk away from a cash register with too much change, every temptation is simply an alternative to meeting God-given needs God's way. Here is how it works. Satan uses your circumstances to stimulate some desire, whether it's a desire for money, sex, or acceptance. Then he starts working on your emotions. Once your emotions have convinced you that you just have to have whatever it is, your mind kicks in. Soon you find yourself working on a plan to meet the need with as few consequences as possible. Then, WHAM! You go for it.

It doesn't matter if you have a problem with gossip, jealousy, anger, gambling, lying, or lust; it's really all the same pattern. Satan hasn't changed his strategy since he tempted Adam and Eve in Eden. He has no need to. If it worked on two perfect people in a perfect environment with a perfect relationship with God, think how much more effective it will be on us—especially if we are unaware of what is going on and have made no provision to stop him.

Stop and think for just a minute. What temptation do you struggle with the most? What is the one that came to mind when I asked this question in the first chapter? Can you see how in one way or another your experience fits this pattern? Let's take it a step further. What God-given need or needs are you being tempted to meet outside of God's parameters? Is it a desire to be loved? A desire to be held? A desire to be accepted? What is it? Before you can go any further, you must know the answer to this question.

Time and time again I have talked to people who were struggling with some area of temptation, but they had no idea why they did the things they did. They felt driven. They knew that their sin brought no long-lasting relief or satisfaction, yet they continued. One good illustration of this is a man I knew who was extremely greedy. To put it another way, every time there was an opportunity to give, he was tempted not to give! He would make all sorts of excuses, none of which were very convincing.

As we talked, it became clear to us that what he really wanted was financial security. He had been raised with nothing and lived with an inordinate fear of poverty. For years he had been greedy and did not even know why. But when he realized that this was his problem and that the Scripture clearly teaches that what we hold on to diminishes and what we let go of multiplies, his attitude began to change.

Anxious for Nothing?

God does not intend for you to live a life full of frustration and anxiety. On the contrary, Satan is the one who wants

[handwritten top margin: 2/13/03 ① "My real need: "Someone to love me unconditionally" — But "Someone" is God!!]

your life to be filled with anxiety. That is why he is always so quick to offer a substitute for God's best. He knows his offer will not satisfy. He also knows that if he can get you hooked on his alternative, many times you will completely miss God's best. *[handwritten margin: can never get that "need" filled by another human being.]*

When I think about the multitude of teenage girls who have compromised their morals in order to be "held," it breaks my heart. They did not need someone just to hold them. They needed someone to love them unconditionally. Many will never know that kind of love simply because they cannot or will not break away from the substitutes Satan has thrown in their path.

Thousands of men and teenage boys in this country are addicted to pornography. For most of them, it all began by accepting Satan's substitute. Now the relationship they really need is beyond their grasp in most cases. Day by day their ability to think about sex and women in the way God intended diminishes.

The alcoholics and drug addicts that fill our streets and occupy positions of prominence are another testimony to the human unwillingness to wait for God's best. For whatever reason, these men and women chose to cope with life's pressures by running. It seemed a quick and easy way to cope. Yet it never solves any of life's problems. It simply postpones the solution. And for many, the pressures that drove them to their vice were the same pressures God was trying to use to drive them to Himself. But they chose the easy way, the quick way, the way of least resistance, the way of destruction.

You see, God does not want you to live a life of frustration and anxiety. If He did, He never could have inspired the apostle Paul to write these words:

Be anxious for nothing, but in everything by prayer and supplication with thanksgiving let your requests be made known to God. And the peace of God, which

[handwritten bottom margin: message ② Wait for God's Best (p.67) Wait for God to provide another solution to the pressure problem]

surpasses all comprehension, shall guard your hearts and minds in Christ Jesus.

—Philippians 4:6–7

The interesting thing about this passage is that God does not promise to give you what you ask for; He does not promise to meet your need immediately. What He promises is "the peace of God," that is, the inner strength to endure until your desires and needs are fulfilled. It will surpass "all comprehension" because the world will look at you and say, "How can you go without _____? How do you make it without _____?" From the world's perspective, it won't make any sense.

My son was thirty before he married. His lost friends used to ask him, "Andy, what do you do about sex?" He would respond, "I wait!" That was amazing from their frame of reference. They could not imagine being "that old" and not being sexually active. The ironic thing was that he was far less frustrated than they were. And so it will always be for those who wait on God to meet their needs His way.

God does not promise to meet your need immediately. But He does promise the inner strength you need to keep going in the meantime. By opting for His peace rather than Satan's substitute, you can be assured that when the time comes for God to meet your particular need, you will be ready.

This principle applies to everything from meeting the right marriage partner to finding the money you need to pay the rent. God knows your needs; He knows your desires. Jesus said,

If you then, being evil, know how to give good gifts to your children, how much more shall your Father who is in heaven give what is good to those who ask Him!

—Matthew 7:11

What an incredible promise! What an incredible God!

Peace at a Price

In all my years as a pastor I have never met one person who waited on God and was sorry. Yet the majority of people who come to my office for counseling or to the counseling offices of our church have problems stemming from a point in their lives where they settled for Satan's substitute. The story is always the same. Things were fine for a while, but before long, they grew restless. Many have made peace with God. Some are still out there bouncing around between jobs, marriages, lovers, and bars. Yet they know in their hearts that they will never find what they are ultimately looking for until they surrender to the One who holds it all in His hands.

What do you really need? What has Satan fooled you into thinking you need? Are you willing to wait and trust God to meet your needs His way? If so, you too can experience the peace that surpasses comprehension.

The remaining chapters of this book are designed to help you deal with Satan's attempts to pull you back into the sin that you have struggled to overcome. You may find some more helpful than others. Depending on the nature of your particular sin, you may need to read certain sections more than once. Whatever the case, do not give up. Peace can be yours if only you will continually take your struggle to God. Ask Him to lift your burden and flood your heart with the peace He has promised.

12/20/02

Ask (God) to lift yr burden and flood your heart w/ the peace He has promised. (and to Renew yr mind w/ His Truth

PART II

DEVELOPING
A
SELF-DEFENSE

CHAPTER·6

Our Great Defender

A WISE INDIVIDUAL prepares for those things that are inevitable in life. Temptation is one of those inevitable things. A plaque I saw not long ago summed it up this way:

OPPORTUNITY ONLY KNOCKS ONCE, TEMPTATION
LEANS ON THE DOORBELL.

Whoever came up with that saying certainly could see the big picture. In this life we will always be within arm's reach of temptation. As we have seen, the Scriptures teach that temptation is common to all men and women everywhere. That being the case, we should do all we can to be prepared.

A general whose task is to defend a city against attack doesn't wait until the city is being besieged to plan his defense. A wise general plans his defense strategy long before the threat of attack even presents itself. "How will the enemy attack? From which direction will they approach? Where are our weak spots?" These are some of the questions a general should ask when preparing his defenses. Likewise believers should sit down ahead of time and plan their defense against temptation.

In these next chapters we are going to take an indepth look at how to develop a self-defense. Step by step I'm going to explain what God would have us do to prepare to combat temptation. This chapter and the next one will focus primarily on God's part, that is, the provision He has made available to us for dealing with temptation. The other chapters in this section will focus on our role. Every stage of this defense strategy is crucial. You may need to read some of these chapters several times, but keep in mind that simply reading this book will not help you in your struggle against temptation. You must apply these principles to make a difference in your life.

God, Our Defender

As we have seen in previous chapters, God has not abandoned us here on earth to struggle through life on our own, nor does He expect us to bear the burden of temptation alone. One of the most exciting truths that surfaces in a study of temptation is that God is intimately involved in the life of every single believer. This will become even more apparent as we focus on the part He plays in our defense against temptation.

When he wrote the Corinthian church, the apostle Paul gave the believers there a warning and a promise concerning temptation. In his promise there are two principles that give us some insight into God's involvement in our defense against temptation. He said,

> Therefore let him who thinks he stands take heed lest he fall. No temptation has overtaken you but such as is common to man; and God is faithful, who will not allow you to be tempted beyond what you are able, but with the temptation will provide the way of escape also, that you may be able to endure it.
> —1 Corinthians 10:12–13

Loving Limitations

The first principle that surfaces in this passage is this: *God has set a limit on the intensity of every temptation.* God knows you perfectly, inside and out. In accordance with His perfect knowledge He has set a limit on the intensity of the temptations you will face. He knows how much you can handle; He knows your breaking point. Regardless of the nature of your temptation—be it in the area of finances, sex, anger, or gossip—God knows your limitations. He promises to keep a watchful eye on the pressures Satan brings against you.

Scripture presents several examples of this. One of the most dramatic is found in Luke when the disciples were gathered with Christ for His last Passover meal. At one point in the dialogue Jesus turned to Peter and said,

> Simon, Simon, behold, Satan has demanded permission to sift you like wheat; but I prayed for you, that your faith may not fail; and you, when once you have turned again, strengthen your brothers.
>
> —Luke 22:31–32

A significant point in this passage is that Satan had to get "permission" to tempt Peter, and he had to demand it. This, however, in no way negates the fact that God determined whether or not Satan would have the chance to tempt Peter the way he did. Before Satan could go after Peter, he first had to check it out with God.

In the same way, God determines how far Satan can go with us. We are not at his mercy. Satan, like all creatures, is ultimately under God's authority. We usually don't think of him in that way. When it comes to temptation, we oftentimes equate God and Satan. We view them as two giant powers battling it out for possession of the universe. The war for the universe, however, ended long ago. Now the battle is for the possession and corruption of men's souls.

The fact that God has put limitations on our temptation assures us of three things. First, we will never be tempted more than we can bear—never! Not in our weakest moments; not even when we are tempted in our weakest areas. Second, God is involved in our struggle against temptation. He isn't watching from a distance. He is right here functioning as referee to the whole situation. Third, God is faithful; He can be trusted. Even in our darkest hour of temptation, God has not turned His back on us. No matter how we respond, God remains faithful. In both our victories and defeats, He continues to keep the enemy in check.

In order to build an effective defense system, you must accept this simple premise. To reject it or simply forget it is to open the door for all kinds of excuses: "I can't help it." "The devil made me do it." "There was no way I could say no." As long as you believe you are at the mercy of the devil when it comes to temptation, you will never know victory because you will never make more than a halfhearted attempt. After all, why try if the temptation is unbearable to begin with?

Imagine a city whose citizens were convinced that no matter what measures they took, their enemies would eventually overrun their walls. What defensive measures do you think they would take? Probably very few or none at all. Why waste their time? They would probably just surrender without a fight.

Satan has many believers convinced that it is a waste of time to try to resist temptation. They believe it is only a matter of time and they will fall. Why go through the frustration of trying if failure is unavoidable? So they surrender without a fight.

That attitude can develop if you do not accept the fact that *God puts a limit on the intensity of your temptation*. Despite your past experience, you must accept by faith that God will not allow you to be tempted beyond what you are able to bear. Think about it. Since you have been a Christian, every temptation you have faced thus far could have been overcome. The same is true for the temptations you face from now on. No matter how difficult this may be to comprehend, you must accept this premise if you are to build an effective defense against the enemy.

The Way Out

The second principle that you must accept if you are going to develop an effective defense against temptation is this: *alongside every temptation, God has designed a way out.* Although the situation may seem hopeless at the time, there is a way to avoid falling. Paul wrote,

> God is faithful, who will not allow you to be tempted beyond what you are able, but with the temptation *will provide the way of escape also,* that you may be able to endure it.
>
> —1 Corinthians 10:13, emphasis added

Someone may say, "I already know of a temptation I am going to face tomorrow!" If that is the case, then you can rest assured that God has already provided a way of escape. Notice the way Paul parallels his ideas: ". . . *with* the temptation will provide the way of escape." Every temptation has an accompanying escape hatch. There is always an alternative action.

Many people live or work in situations where they are constantly being tempted to sin. Oftentimes there is no place or opportunity for them to run. God is faithful even in those situations. He will always provide a way out.

A girl in our fellowship grew up in such an environment. I'll call her Michele. The nature of her family was such that she and her sister were constantly tempted to rebel in the worst way. Her parents were warned several times by both friends and neighbors that they were driving their girls away.

Eventually Michele's sister ran away and got married. Her decision to marry was more an effort to escape than it was an act of love. Michele, on the other hand, stuck it out all the way through high school and college. I must admit that even I was amazed at her ability to cope with the situation at home. Eventually she fell in love with a fine Christian young man, and I had the opportunity to marry them.

During one of our premarital counseling sessions, the subject of her home life surfaced. In a very tactful way I expressed my respect for her ability to have handled things as well as she did. She smiled and said, "Sometimes you just have to do what you are told and then look for alternatives when you can't." I asked her if she ever felt like rebelling. She said, "All the time. There were days when I just didn't think I could stand it one more minute. I learned that if I would stop, take a deep breath, and think for just a minute, there was always another way to handle the situation other than blowing up." Michele learned that *even when we cannot escape a situation, God always provides a way to escape temptation.*

Our problem may be that we don't bother to look for His way out. We assume the situation is hopeless and just go along with what our flesh is directing us to do. And if we are honest, sometimes we don't look for God's way of escape because we don't really want to escape. If that is your problem, you need to go back and reread the first three chapters of this book. You still don't have the big picture as far as the sin is concerned.

On the other hand, if you sincerely want to escape temptation and you know you are going to face a particular temptation, go ahead and ask God to reveal to you the way out. Remember, a good general doesn't wait until the battle has begun to plan his strategy. He thinks ahead.

I know a pastor in another city who had problems with a woman in his church. She was obviously interested in more than a pastor-parishioner relationship. I'll call her Doris. The pastor did everything he could to avoid her advances. The only situation he could not seem to find a way to deal with occurred after each Sunday morning service. Doris would stand in line with the other church members to greet him, and she would always give him a lingering full frontal hug. Week after week he knew what was coming, and yet he couldn't find a way to avoid her without making a scene. Then one morning he had an idea. Just as it was Doris's turn in line, he reached down and picked up a small child. Holding the child in front of him, he greeted Doris with a handshake from his free hand. From then on when the pastor would see her coming, the Lord was faithful to provide a "way out." There was always a child nearby. After a few weeks, Doris got the message and no longer bothered him in that way.

God will be faithful to provide a way of escape, but we must be faithful to look for it. And having identified it, we must take advantage of it.

"Deliver Us From Evil"

Before we move on, I want to point out what 1 Corinthians 10:13 does *not* say. It does not say that God will remove the temptation. God will not provide a way to escape being tempted. (We may wish that He would, but that's just not the way things are.) The point of this verse is that He will provide an alternative course of action. God's ultimate desire for us is not that we should be delivered from being tempted, but that we should be delivered through temptation. Notice how this verse ends:

> But with the temptation will provide the way of escape also, *that you may be able to endure it*.

God's desire for us is that we should be able to endure, or bear, temptation.

When Jesus was praying in the Garden of Gethsemane before His arrest, He prayed,

> I have given them Thy word; and the world has hated them, because they are not of the world, even as I am

not of the world. I do not ask Thee to take them out of
the world, but to keep them from the evil one.
—John 17:14–15

Jesus specifically mentioned that it was not His desire for the
disciples to be taken out of the world and therefore avoid all
temptation. His desire for them was that they remain in the
world, but at the same time be protected from Satan, the evil
one. In other words, "Give them the power to overcome the
onslaught of the devil." Part of God's answer to His Son's
prayer is "the way of escape."

I stress this point in view of our tendency to feel as if
God has somehow let us down when we are tempted.
"God, if You really love me, if You really care for me, why are
You allowing me to be tempted this way?" But nowhere does
God promise to structure our lives so that we can avoid all
temptation. He does, however, limit our temptations and
provide us a way out.

Promises, Promises

In this chapter we have focused on the first part of
God's provision for our defense against temptation. God
stands guard over Satan when he tempts us. He will not allow us to be tempted beyond what we can bear. Second,
with every temptation God provides a way of escape. It is
our responsibility to look for it and take advantage of it.

The awesome implication of both principles is that
God is intimately involved in our lives. He is aware of every
temptation we face. Before you read any further, stop and
answer these two questions for yourself:

1. Do I really believe God only allows me to be tempted
   within the confines of what He knows I can bear?
2. Do I really believe God provides a way of escape
   through every temptation?

If you have trouble accepting these two premises, please take some time to meditate on 1 Corinthians 10:13. Ask God to make this verse real to you. Think through the experiences you have had that make this verse so unbelievable. Ask God to help you reinterpret your experiences from His perspective. In the next chapter we will take a look at two other ways in which God has involved Himself in helping us develop a defense against temptation.

CHAPTER 7

The Power of His Might

THERE IS A third aspect to God's involvement in our temptations. He limits our temptations and provides a way to escape, and *He also provides us with the power to overcome*. Of all the concepts discussed in this book, this one is the most difficult to explain. The very term *power* introduces an intangible into our discussion. Power is not something that can be seen. Power is something that is applied. After properly applying power to a situation, one can see the results of power, yet the power itself remains as illusive as ever.

Wind is a good example of this. You cannot see wind. Yet you can readily see the results of wind. If you have ever driven through an area immediately following a hurricane or tornado, you know firsthand what I'm talking about. A tornado passed through the neighborhood of a family in our church several years ago. Their roof was torn completely off, and all the windows were shattered. Right next to their house was a huge magnolia tree. It must have been twenty feet high. The power of the tornado was of such great magnitude that it ripped up the magnolia tree by the roots and carried it away. They never found a trace of the tree! Every time I see the place where that tree once stood I can't help wondering where it eventually landed. Such is the nature of power. Rarely seen, always felt.

We need to keep in mind three things about power. I'll refer to these as the "laws of power." First, *power deter-*

mines potential. The potential weight a bodybuilder can lift is limited by his strength or power. Certainly his attitude is important, but even a good attitude does not compensate for a lack of power. Our potential to accomplish any particular task, whether it is moving something heavy or saying no to temptation, is determined by the power we possess or to which we have access. Power determines potential.

Second, *power must be harnessed and applied toward a specific goal before it serves any purpose*. Power in and of itself is useless. Its value lies in its application. The Colorado River has a great deal of potential power. It is not until the force of the river comes into contact with the turbines underneath the Hoover Dam, however, that the power of the Colorado River serves any useful function. Power must be applied. Setting a chain saw down by a tree accomplishes nothing. There may be no doubt in anyone's mind that the potential for cutting down the tree is there. Nothing will be accomplished, however, until someone comes along and applies the power of the saw to the tree. Power must be harnessed to be useful.

Third, *power, when harnessed and focused, can greatly extend the potential of the one in whose hands the power rests*. When individuals have access to a source of power beyond what they possess themselves, there is a sense in which that power becomes theirs. Yet at the same time there remains a distinction. The potential of the one to whom control has been given is greatly enhanced. If you were to ask a man holding a chain saw, "Can you cut down this tree in ten minutes?" he would probably reply, "Sure!" He knows that with the power the chain saw affords him, he can cut down the tree. He does not mean that he can cut down the tree with his bare hands. Power becomes an extension of the one who controls and directs it.

The Promise of Power

Keeping all this in mind, think about the implications of this passage:

Finally, be strong in the Lord, and in the strength of His might. Put on the full armor of God, that you may be able to stand firm against the schemes of the devil.
—Ephesians 6:10–11

Those verses made two very important points to the Ephesians—and they still pertain to us. First, a power was available to the Ephesian believers that was not of them. Paul exhorted the Ephesians to be strong in the strength, or power, of "His" might. Second, when the power was properly harnessed and focused, the Ephesian believers would be able to stand firmly against any of the devil's schemes.

Paul made the same point in Romans when he wrote,

So then, brethren, we are under obligation, not to the flesh, to live according to the flesh.
—Romans 8:12

To state it another way, "Brethren, you have the *power* to say no to your fleshly desires." In the same book he said,

For sin shall not be master over you, for you are not under law, but under grace.
—Romans 6:14

In those verses Paul was teaching something really amazing, especially in light of the way believers often live. The truth Paul was getting at can be stated this way: *believers have a power greater than that of the devil, the flesh, or sin*. Believers have the potential to say no to the devil, no to the flesh, and no to sin! And not once did Paul qualify his statements; there are no exceptions.

Probably the most important role God plays when we are tempted is that of *empowerer*. God has made available to us the power, His power, to say no to sin and yes to Him. Regardless of the intensity of our temptation, the frequency of our temptation, or even our failure in the past to success-fully deal with it, God has made available the power to re-sist.

Seeing Is Believing

Someone may respond, "Well, if God has given me all this power, why do I keep giving in to the same tempta-tions over and over? I pray and ask God to help me, but nothing changes!" It was in anticipation of this very re-sponse that I took the time to describe the three laws of power earlier. The second law stated that *power must be har-nessed and applied toward a specific goal before it serves any pur-pose*. Remember, power in and of itself is useless. Its value is in its application. *Having* the power of God available and *us-ing* that power are two entirely different things. A believer who is unable to say no to sin is like a man who owns a chain saw but is attempting to chop down trees with his bare hands. He has the potential through the chain saw, but he is not using it. Owning a chain saw with the potential power to cut down trees is not the same thing as sawing down trees. Having the power of God at your disposal is not equivalent to overcoming temptation.

This is exactly what James is talking about when he writes,

> What use is it, my brethren, if a man says he has faith, but he has no works? Can that faith save him?
> —James 2:14

And then a few verses later he writes,

> But are you willing to recognize, you foolish fellow, that faith, without works is useless?
> —James 2:20

James's point is that faith apart from the application of that faith is useless; it accomplishes nothing; it might as well not even be there! The application of faith or power makes things happen. Practically speaking, there is really no value at all in having the power of God residing in you if you are not putting it to use. It's like owning a car and keeping it parked in the garage all the time. What use is it? A believer's inability to cope with a particular temptation is in no way a reflection on the power of God; only the individual's inability or unwillingness to apply that power becomes evident.

I was in the ministry for years before I began to understand my relationship to the power of God. I knew that God had made His power available, but for a long time I did not know how to make it a reality in my own life. Most of the Christians that I counsel have the same problem. They believe victory is possible, but not very probable. The remaining portion of this book is dedicated to explaining how to make the power of God a reality, how to get God's power working for you.

A Change for the Better

Before we get to that, however, let's examine a fourth aspect of God's involvement in our temptations. This one has to do with the *changes that took place in our relationship to sin and our relationship with God the moment we trusted Him as our Savior*. The realization of these two things really paved the way for me to begin experiencing consistent victory in my life. As a child, I had been taught some things that were incorrect; they were so deeply ingrained in my thinking that without knowing it, I read them back into the Scripture. When the truth finally broke through, however, and my perspective was brought into line with God's, I found it far easier to apply the power of God to my particular temptations.

Dead to Sin

The Bible says that each of us is born under the dominion of sin (Rom. 5:17-19). Through the desires of the flesh, the power of sin directs a man's or woman's actions and attitudes. The power of sin functions much like an internal dictator. Its commands flow from a desire to fulfill every desire and meet every immediate need in whatever fashion it deems appropriate. The power of sin knows no rules, for it functions as a law unto itself. Therefore, it eventually comes into conflict with any standard of behavior, whether it is social, legal, or biblical.

The power of sin is that innate desire within each of us to assert ourselves against our Creator or authority in general. The power of sin causes us to resent being asked to go out of our way for someone else. No doubt at some point in your life you have been told to do something and immediately felt something spring up inside that made you want to lash out at the one giving the command. That is the power of sin. It tends to make itself heard in statements like these: "I don't want to!" "Do it yourself!" "Give it to me!" "I did the work, not him!" "I don't care what you think!" "Don't tell me what to do!" This is the way sin responds to authority—God's, the government's, or your employer's.

The power of sin oftentimes drives us to sin. It is the force we battle when we are tempted. It is that extra entity within that seems to always push us in the opposite direction from which we know God would have us go. The power of sin is so real that biblical authors personified it. When he was describing Cain's anger toward his brother Abel, Moses wrote,

Then the LORD said to Cain, "Why are you angry? And why has your countenance fallen? If you do well, will not your countenance be lifted up? And if you do not do well, *sin is crouching at the door;* and its desire is for you, but you must master it."

—Genesis 4:6–7

The power of sin is described here as a wild beast waiting to devour its prey. That is exactly how the power of sin operates. It waits for just the right opportunity to leap out and destroy our relationships, homes, thoughts, and self-esteem. The power of sin expresses itself in most cases as an attitude of rebellion. It can be as extreme as the declaration: "I don't care what is the right thing to do; I'm going to _____." Or it can be expressed in more subtle ways: "I know I should _____, but I don't want to." Or "I know I should _____, but I just can't." Usually "I can't" really means "I won't." In each case the power of sin has won out over what is right.

The apostle Paul described his battle with sin in these terms:

> For we know that the Law is spiritual; but I am of flesh, sold into bondage to sin. For that which I am doing, I do not understand; for I am not practicing what I would like to do, but I am doing the very thing I hate. But if I do the very thing I do not wish to do, I agree with the Law, confessing that it is good. So now, no longer am I the one doing it, but sin which indwells me. . . . I find then the principle that evil is present in me, the one who wishes to do good.
>
> —Romans 7:14–17, 21

All of us have experienced a similar struggle. We know what we should do; at times we even want to do it; but we cannot find it within ourselves to do what is right. Nonbelievers do not have the power to consistently overcome the power of sin in their lives. For them, it is a futile struggle. For believers, however, it is a different story.

Do You Not Know?

Now here comes the part that took me years to really understand. The Scripture teaches that believers are "dead" to the power of sin. Paul wrote,

What shall we say then? Are we to continue in sin that grace might increase? May it never be! How shall we who *died to sin* still live in it? Or do you not know that all of us who have been baptized into Christ Jesus have been baptized into His death?
—Romans 6:1–3, emphasis added

Then a few verses later:

Even so consider yourselves to be dead to sin, but alive to God in Christ Jesus.
—Romans 6:11

When Paul used the term *dead* in relationship to sin, he meant that sin no longer has the power to force us to do or think anything. But he did not mean that the power of sin no longer exists as an influence. The power of sin has *access* to us but no *authority* over us. Unfortunately, it is difficult sometimes to distinguish between the two. This is especially true for those who become believers later in life.

Several years ago a friend of the family gave us a schnauzer puppy. We named him Rommel. While Rommel was still a puppy, my son, Andy, put a collar around his neck and proceeded to teach him how to sit down, lie down, and shake hands. The way he did this was by saying, "Sit, Rommel!" Then he pushed the puppy's rear down while yanking his collar up to force Rommel into the appropriate position. Once this process was complete, Andy would reward Rommel with something to eat. This went on for days. Then he went through similar steps with the other commands. Finally, all Andy had to do was walk up to Rommel and say, "Sit," and Rommel would sit. "Lie down," and he would lie down. "Shake hands," and he would shake hands. There was no yanking on his collar or even a reward for his performance. Yet for the rest of his life, Rommel responded immediately to those three commands.

There is a sense in which Satan has a collar around the neck of each unbeliever. That collar is called the power of sin. When Satan says, "Lie," the power of sin yanks the unbeliever toward lying. When the unbeliever has an impure thought, the power of sin fastens his attention on that thought. When an unbeliever is given an order, the power of sin focuses her attention on her right to do whatever she pleases. An unbeliever can resist the power of sin, but eventually he will give in.

When a person becomes a Christian, God removes the collar. That is what it means to be dead to sin. Satan can still give commands. And impure thoughts may still flash through one's mind. Thoughts of independence may still surface on occasion. The difference is that the believer is free to choose against these things. The power of sin has been broken. Satan and the flesh still have access to the mind, but they have no authority over the will. The believer is free to choose. The believer is free to say no.

The problem may be that, like Rommel, you are so used to responding a certain way that you give in without a fight. You think, *What's the use? I've done it a thousand times. There is no use struggling; this is just the way I am.* Wrong! That is not the way you *are*; that is the way you have *chosen* to be. Regardless of how you feel, regardless of what you have done in the past, God says that once you have trusted Christ as your Savior, you are free from the power of sin.

After we took the collar off Rommel, he never *had* to obey us again. From then on, he freely *chose* to obey. Once the power of sin has been broken in your life, you never have to obey the desires of the flesh, the commands of the devil, or the call of the world. You are free to choose. The problem oftentimes is that your past experience has conditioned you. You expect to fall to certain temptations. By applying the principles outlined in this book, however, you can recondition yourself. The Bible calls this renewing your mind. We will deal with that in more detail in a later chapter. For now, you must accept the truth that the power of sin has been broken. What you do is a matter of choice.

Alive to God

Dying to sin is only half the story. The other half is that believers are alive to God. Paul wrote,

> For the death that He [Christ] died, He died to sin, once for all; but the life that He lives, He lives to God. Even so consider yourselves to be dead to sin, but alive to God in Christ Jesus.
>
> —Romans 6:10–11

Not only did our relationship to sin change, but our relationship with God changed as well. Now this may seem elementary at first. We know our relationship with God changed when we trusted Christ, but we may not know how it changed and to what extent it changed. And if we do not have this knowledge, the power of sin will continue to have an influence.

Paul knew this to be the case. In fact, his whole discussion of the believer's relationship to sin and with God is introduced with a question: "Or do you not know . . . ?" (Rom. 6:3). He knew that believers who were still living under the influence of the power of sin had not yet come to grips with the unique changes in their relationship with God. So at the risk of insulting their intelligence or covering old territory, he explained it again:

Or do you not know that all of us who have been baptized into Christ Jesus have been baptized into His
death? Therefore we have been buried with Him
through baptism into death, in order that as Christ was
raised from the dead through the glory of the Father, so
we too might walk in newness of life. For if we have
become united with Him in the likeness of His death,
certainly we shall be also in the likeness of His resurrection, knowing this, that our old self was crucified with
Him, that our body of sin might be done away with,
that we should no longer be slaves to sin; for he who
died is freed from sin.

—Romans 6:3–7

When you trusted Christ as your Savior, the Bible
says you were "baptized into Christ." In our culture that
phrase communicates little or nothing, but in Paul's day it
meant a great deal. The term *baptize* literally means "to im-
merse something into something else." In Bible days they
would *baptize* a piece of cloth into dye in order to change its
color. We would say "dip."

The term *baptize* had a figurative meaning as well. A
study of first-century literature reveals that this figurative
meaning of the term was used more often than the literal
meaning. The figurative meaning of the term *baptize* had to
do with the concept of identification. For instance, if Gentiles
(non-Jews) wanted to join the Jewish faith, they would go
through a series of rituals that would culminate with their
baptism. The custom was for them to dip themselves under
water. This signified a transformation from whatever form of
religion they had embraced to Judaism. The act of baptism
represented death to the old way of life and resurrection to a
new way of life. The baptism was an outward expression of
an inward decision to identify with the Jewish race and religion. Now, practically, all that was true of a Jew would be

true of them. The Jewish God would be their God. Enemies of the Jews would now be their enemies. They would assume Jewish customs, dress, and eating habits. For all practical purposes, they had become Jewish.

A Family Affair

When Paul speaks of believers as having been baptized into Christ, he means we have been identified with Christ to the degree that what is true of Him becomes true of us. The legal ramifications of adoption in our culture closely parallel this concept. Imagine for a moment a married couple who for medical reasons is unable to have children. Several years into their marriage they win $10 million in a lottery. The following year they adopt a son. The papers are drawn up in such a fashion as to give him all the rights of a natural son. Thus, he is the heir to all his parents own. Now think about this situation.

QUESTION: How much is the son worth?

ANSWER: As much as the parents.

QUESTION: Was the adopted son *actually* there when they won the money?

ANSWER: No!

QUESTION: Is it *actually,* legally his?

ANSWER: Yes.

QUESTION: When did it become his?

ANSWER: When he was legally placed into the family.

The truth Paul wants you to understand is that when you became a Christian, you were placed into God's family through adoption. God baptized or identified or adopted (however you want to look at it) you into Christ. Therefore, what is true of Christ, in respect to what has happened to Him in the past, is true of you!

What happened to Christ? He was put to death. Since we are in Christ now, we have all the benefits of a Person who was put to death. Thus, Paul wrote that we "have been baptized into His death" (Rom. 6:3). In the same vein he continued,

> Therefore we have been buried with Him through baptism into death, in order that as Christ was raised from the dead through the glory of the Father, so we too might walk in newness of life.
>
> —Romans 6:4

Were we *actually* there when Christ was put to death and raised from the dead? No. Do we *actually* have the benefits of One who was put to death and raised from the dead? Yes! And what is the benefit of being identified with Christ's death and resurrection?

> For the death that He died, He died to sin, once for all; but the life that He lives, He lives to God.
>
> —Romans 6:10

Christ died to sin. Since we have been identified with Christ, we too are actually dead to sin. So Paul continued,

> Even so consider yourselves to be dead to sin, but alive to God in Christ Jesus.
>
> —Romans 6:11

We have the same relationship to sin that Christ had. What is even better, we have the same rights of relationship with God that Christ has. We are alive to God!

Making it Work

This truth may sound utterly ridiculous in light of your experience. You might ask, " How can I be 'dead' to sin and alive to God and act the way I do?" Simple. Remember the second law of power: *power must be harnessed and applied toward a specific goal before it serves any purpose*. Until you apply these truths to your specific situation, you will continue to respond like a dog on a leash. Every time you feel those old feelings creeping in you will reach for whatever you have been conditioned to reach for in order to temporarily quench that desire. You must accept that God has set the stage for you to experience victory over the temptations plaguing your life. He has placed you into Christ. You are a brand-new person. You have the benefits of actually having died to the power of sin. You are tapped in to the life and power of God. It is time you began putting that power to work.

The following chapters focus on making this simple principle a reality. However, until you are able to accept this final premise as reality, you will probably find very little lasting help from this book. The starting point for lasting victory over sin is accepting the fact that you are dead to the power of sin. Satan, the flesh, and the world may stand on the sidelines and scream for your attention, but they cannot force you to do anything. That power has been broken. Christ's death on the cross broke once and for all the power of sin. The collar has been removed.

Second, you are alive to God. His power resides in you. The power that raised Christ from the dead is available to you every day. This is the same power that moved Christ through this life without His once giving in to temptation. If you will put it to use, you too can move through your days and nights in victory.

A Simple Suggestion

As you continue through the principles outlined in the following chapters, let me encourage you to begin doing one thing. Meditate on this simple statement: "I am dead to sin and alive to God." Repeat it over and over under your breath as you go about your daily activities. When you are tempted, say it out loud. Sing it out loud as you drive. Write it down on an index card and place it where you can see it every day. Scribble it on your notepad during meetings. Use every opportunity during the day to get this simple yet life-changing principle ingrained into your mind. When you feel those old feelings creeping in, speak it out loud, "I may feel the way I used to feel, but the truth is that I am dead to sin and alive to God."

I'll never forget what a professor of mine once told a new convert, "You cannot live the way you used to live, for you are not the person you used to be." That is the truth. It is my prayer in closing this chapter that the truth of that statement will become a reality in your experience.

CHAPTER 8

Avoiding the Danger Zones

CHUCK WAS A successful young attorney. Along with his wife and new baby, he rarely missed a church service. He had been raised in a fine Christian home, and for the most part he had walked with God throughout both college and law school. But one afternoon Chuck made a decision that eventually cost him his family and his job.

Chuck's firm needed another paralegal secretary, and he was assigned the responsibility of interviewing the applicants and hiring one of them. The second woman he interviewed seemed like the perfect choice. She had several years of experience as well as a pleasant personality. Chuck was so impressed he considered cancelling the other interviews. But he realized that would be somewhat unfair to the women who had already made appointments, so he chose to continue with the interviews.

Chuck was in a great mood as he got out of his car Thursday morning and began walking toward his office. That morning he would conduct his last interview and then get on with his "real" job. As he reached for the door, he noticed in the reflection on the glass that a woman was walking up behind him. Politely, he opened the door and waited for her to enter first. He couldn't help noticing that she was a very attractive young lady. Without thinking about it he watched her walk ahead of him to the elevator. He followed her into the elevator, thinking, *There is certainly nothing wrong with riding in the elevator with a beautiful woman. Besides, it's the only one available.*

"Four, please," she said. Chuck quickly pushed the button for the fourth floor. He grinned. That was his floor. Then the thought occurred to him, *Is this the woman who is interviewing?* And of course she was.

The interview went well, considering the fact that Chuck had a difficult time keeping his mind on what she was saying rather than on how she looked. Something inside kept saying, "There is no way you can hire her." At the same time his well-trained, analytical mind kept responding, "But it will enhance the image of the office to have an attractive young lady around. Besides, the fact that she has very little experience will make it easier for us to train her to our way of doing things. There is nothing wrong with hiring her." In the end his reason reigned, and Joyce became the firm's new paralegal.

As time passed Chuck began paying more and more attention to Joyce. For the first time in his career he actually looked forward to Secretary's Day. He spent over an hour looking for just the right card to give her. The whole time a little warning kept popping up in his conscience, "Chuck, back off." But he would always have a good reason for everything he did, "She has worked hard. I need to show her my appreciation." Soon other people in the office began to notice the extra attention Chuck paid to her. Every once in a while someone would say something about it. Chuck would smile and say, "There is nothing wrong with . . . ," and excuse whatever it was that had been brought up.

Lunch became a regular thing for Chuck and Joyce. Then it was dinner after work. The gifts continued and began to increase in size and value. All the while Chuck told himself, "There is nothing wrong with showing my appreciation. There is nothing wrong with eating out with my secretary."

It wasn't long before Joyce's professional admiration for her boss became a romantic attraction. One thing led to another, as it almost always does, and what ensued was an adulterous relationship that neither Chuck nor Joyce anticipated.

What Happened?

Chuck's story is one that has been repeated thousands of times with different people in different circumstances. In fact, as you read his story I'm sure you anticipated the ending; it came as no surprise. As common and predictable as this story may be, I want us to analyze it because it carries with it all the ingredients that make for disaster in all of our lives.

Like many of us, Chuck followed this line of reasoning about sin: "There are right things, and there are wrong things. My goal as a Christian is to always stay on the right side of things. As long as I do that, everything will be fine. As long as something is not clearly wrong, it is permissible." So every time he felt a little hesitant about his relationship with Joyce he could dismiss it by saying, "But I'm not doing anything wrong." And by his way of looking at things, he was exactly right.

We all have a tendency to think this way. We have a line drawn in our minds that separates right from wrong. As long as we are on the right side of things, we feel as if everything is all right. And should someone try to warn us about something, we may become defensive and say, "I'm not doing anything wrong! The Bible doesn't say anything about this."

Along with this way of thinking comes another tendency. That is to move as close to the line of sin as we can without actually sinning. For instance, when we see a policeman somewhere in the traffic behind us and we are in a 55-mile-per-hour speed zone, what speed do we slow down to?

Usually right down to the line, 55. That is the way we think.

High-school students often express the same way of thinking with this question, "How far can my steady and I go?" What they are really asking in most cases is, "Exactly where is the line between what is permissible and what is not? After you tell us, we are going to camp out right on the line!" We want to go as far as we can; we want to know how close we can get to sin without actually sinning. This question is constantly being asked of relationships, tax deductions, speed limits, expense accounts, rock music, dancing, and anything else where there is a margin of vagueness.

Unfortunately there will never be an agreed-upon biblical answer for these "grey areas." The Bible doesn't address itself to the question of how far a person can go toward sin without actually sinning. That was never a concern of the biblical authors as they wrote. Moved by the Holy Spirit, they were addressing an entirely different question, "How can I become more Christlike in my character? How can I be used to encourage those around me to become more like Christ?" Those were the concerns of the biblical writers.

The problem with wanting to know how close to sin we can get without sinning is that the motivation behind the question is such that once we find a satisfactory answer we immediately position ourselves on the edge of moral or ethical disaster. We develop lifestyles so close to the edge that Satan has to do very little to push us over into sin.

The Calorie-Conscious Counselor

Imagine for a moment that a friend of yours complained to you about his inability to stay on his diet. Being a concerned friend, you ask him when he finds it most difficult. What would you think if he replied, "I do pretty good until I go into the ice-cream shop, order a hot fudge sundae, and put a big spoonful right in front of my mouth. Every time I do that I just can't resist the temptation"? Not very bright, huh?

Let's take it one step further. Without losing your cool you share with him that if he is really serious about staying on his diet, he needs to stay out of the ice-cream shop. How would you feel if he responded, "There's nothing wrong with going into the ice-cream shop! People do it all the time. I even saw the pastor and his wife in the ice-cream shop. You are so legalistic"?

Well, he has a point. There is nothing wrong with going into an ice-cream shop. But he is missing another point, isn't he? He is missing the point that many Christians miss when it comes to successfully dealing with temptation. When we are faced with decisions about opportunities, invitations, vacations, gifts, movies, music, books, magazines, videos, dates, or anything else that pertains to our daily lives, we shouldn't be asking, "What's wrong with this?" Instead we should be asking, "What is the wise thing to do?"

Walking Wisely

When he wrote to the believers in Ephesus, Paul concluded a lengthy discussion concerning issues of right and wrong with this admonition:

> Therefore be careful how you walk, not as unwise men, but as wise.
>
> —Ephesians 5:15

The relationship between Paul's exhortation here and the verses that preceded it cannot be overemphasized. The term *therefore* communicates the idea of, "Now if you're serious about following through with what I have just said . . ." Paul had just described how believers are to respond to those whose lives could be described as immoral, greedy, impure, covetous, or crude. He instructed them not to "participate" with them. He even encouraged them to go so far as to "expose" what those people were up to. At that point he shifted his discussion to the issue of wisdom. His point is clear. If we are to stay untainted by the sinful people we rub shoulders with every day, we must learn to walk wisely.

Scope It Out!

As Paul used the phrase here, *be careful* meant to "examine carefully." He was saying that in all of life we must scope out each opportunity and situation carefully; we must weigh the pros and the cons. We must get in the habit of testing each opportunity in light of our past experience, present weaknesses, and future plans. My experience as a pastor tells me that people rarely plan to get into trouble. Their problem is that they fail to plan to stay out of trouble.

In terms of one's past experience, wisdom asks, "What happened the last time I was involved with this group?" "What usually happens when I go to this place?" Wisdom does not rationalize, "There's nothing wrong with those people." That is not the issue. The issue concerns the wisdom of your going out with them.

Like most pastors, I have seen countless young people and single adults go down the drain morally. For many couples I could see it coming a mile off. Time and time again I have warned people or had members of my staff warn them. And over and over again we get the same routine. A young man or woman will defend the relationship based on the partner's overall character or background while ignoring the fact that the relationship is outside God's parameters and that past experience indicates it will stay that way as long as they are together.

They say things like, "But you don't understand. He is a great guy. He is so polite and sensitive." Or "She is the finest girl I've ever dated. Sure we have our problems, but she has so much going for her. I would be a fool to drop her." And so they continue outside God's will, promising over and over again that things will change until the bottom drops out. These relationships are usually short-lived. Finally, one of the two will lose interest in the other. Or the girl may get pregnant. Either way, there is a great deal of hurt. They always wish they had listened.

What About Now?

Wisdom makes decisions in light of the past, and it is also sensitive to present weaknesses. By present weaknesses, I am referring to the fact that we are more susceptible to certain temptations at some times than at others. For instance, right after teenagers have a big argument with their parents, they are usually more prone to do things they would normally not do. I have talked to kids who took their first drink right after a big blowup at home. They were not sure why they did it. They just felt "extra rebellious" as one boy put it.

A businessman who has just landed a big deal that he has worked for weeks or months to put together may be more vulnerable than normal to certain temptations. When a man experiences a great deal of success, he sometimes feels as if he owes it to himself to take some extra liberties. Sometimes he feels above the law.

People who are committed to walking wisely stay in touch with their feelings and frustrations. They realize that what may have been safe last weekend could possibly lead to disaster this weekend; that what was easy to resist last night may be more difficult to say no to tonight. They approach every opportunity, invitation, and relationship in light of their present state of mind and feelings.

Planning Ahead

The third area wisdom always considers is the future, which includes plans, goals, and dreams. Just about every sin we are tempted to commit has a direct or an indirect effect on our future. Whether it is cheating, lying, stealing, gossiping, or some sort of sexual sin, it touches our future. If we are wise, we will look beyond the immediate pleasure of sin to its ultimate effect on our plans for the future. Therefore, the clearer our goals are, the easier it becomes to say no to temptation. Why? Because one of the lies of Satan is, "This won't hurt a bit!" As we have seen, however, every sin hurts; nobody gets by with sin. Goal-oriented people are more apt to view present decisions in light of future consequences.

A young girl who has purposed in her heart to keep herself morally pure for the man she will eventually marry will have more resolve when tempted to compromise than the girl who has never really given much thought to what kind of woman she wants to be someday. A father who desires to keep his kids on his team once they become teenagers will resist the temptation to constantly busy himself with his own pursuits while his children are young. The wife who has purposed in her heart to keep her marriage exciting will resist the temptation to slack off in her efforts to look pleasing to her husband. The wise person always measures each thought, opportunity, and relationship by its effect on future plans and dreams.

Christians don't wake up one morning and just out of the blue decide to go out and have an affair. Businessmen don't begin their careers with the intent of being dishonest. Singles don't plan dating relationships that will result in an unwanted pregnancy. Families don't plan to go into debt up to their ears. Married couples do not start out planning somewhere down the road to get divorced. I have never met a Christian teenager who planned to drink the first beer. Neither have I met a Christian young lady who set out ahead of time to lose her virginity. Yet all of these things happen every day. Why? Because we don't plan well enough for these things not to happen.

It Is an Evil Day

We live in an age in which everything is working against the things we hold dear. Think about it. What force in our society is working to help you remain faithful to your partner? None that I can think of. The message of our world is just the opposite. What force in our society is working to help your kids remain true to principles the Bible sets forth in regard to sexual purity, honesty, loyalty, and the priority of character development? None! The message our kids are bombarded with is, "Acquire all you can and do whatever feels good." We don't live in a neutral world that beckons us to choose between right and wrong. The world we face every day is one in which right has become wrong.

Believers cannot afford to go out into the world without taking major precautions. Paul lists two things believers should do if they are serious about surviving morally and ethically. The first one is found immediately following the verse we just looked at:

> Therefore be careful how you walk, not as unwise men, but as wise, *making the most of your time*, because the days are evil.
> —Ephesians 5:15–16, emphasis added

Apparently the Ephesian society was not much better off than ours. In fact, in some respects it was worse. In our society immorality is associated with godlessness, but in Ephesus immorality played a central role in the religion of that culture. In their worship of the goddess Artemis, the Ephesians participated in sensual fertility rituals that included orgiastic rites as well as prostitution. Imagine living in a society where religious convictions were demonstrated through immoral conduct!

In addressing the believers of this city, Paul advised

them to make the most of their time. That is, they should use their time carefully. Paul realized that it required absolutely no effort on their part to become like the world. They did not have to study or set goals or even make any plans to become worldly. All they had to do was get out in the world and live. If they took no precautions, it would be just a matter of time before they looked, acted, and thought just like the world. And that applies to us, too.

That being the case, Paul warned the Ephesian believers to take every available moment and work toward reversing this process. To keep from becoming like the world takes a conscious effort, and that means time. It is so easy to become lazy with "extra" time. Yet to do so is really a step toward failure.

The wise father, for instance, does not walk into the house, throw down his briefcase, and plop down in front of the television or pick up the newspaper. He thinks, *I have thirty minutes until dinner. I haven't seen my kids all day. I haven't talked to my wife all day. I'll take this time and invest it in those relationships instead of watching the tube.* Is that to say there is something wrong with watching television after work? Not at all. That is just the point. The question is not one of wrong versus right. It is a matter of choosing the wise thing. Our world crowds out family time. So those who are serious about overcoming the pressures of this world system must take advantage of every spare minute to do so.

The wise housewife does not turn on the television to keep her company while she is cleaning. She thinks instead, *Ah! An hour to choose what I must listen to. What is the wisest thing to fill my mind with? Television? Not hardly.* So she reaches for some Christian music or tapes of sermons or something that will be edifying. Is that to say a housewife must never watch television while she is at home alone? Of course not. But the wise housewife realizes that these are evil days in which we live. She must, therefore, use every spare minute to safeguard against becoming like the world that is working so hard to destroy everything she holds dear.

Wise teenagers or college students do not jump into the car and immediately turn up the radio. As they shut the door, they think, *Silence! For the next few minutes I can control what goes into my head. I can't control it in class. I can't control what I hear in the locker room. I don't even have too much control at home. But for now I can decide.* Instead of pumping in more error from the radio, wise students use that time to fill their minds with something good for a change. And again, the issue is not whether Christians should listen to the radio! The issue has to do with the wisest way to use precious spare time.

You may be thinking, *What has all of this got to do with temptation?* Simply this. One of Satan's tricks is to keep our minds off the truth for extended periods of time. During this time he slowly leads our thinking and our emotions further and further away from the truth. Then when we are least expecting it, WHAM! We fall. That is why we are so vulnerable during vacation. We get out of our routine. We let the spiritual disciplines go for a while. We go for hours and even days without any direct reminders of what is true and right. Our emotions grow more sensitive to the things of the world rather than the things of God. And then we wonder how we slip so easily into sin, sin we would never have considered at home.

In this evil day in which we live we need constant reminders of the truth. If we are not careful with our time, we will allow others to fill it up for us. There will be no time for God. Consequently, we will be set up to fall. Wise men and women are careful with their time. They use their extra time to draw close to God; to check themselves out; to make sure they are not creeping ever so slowly toward that illusive line dividing things that are of God from things that are of the world.

Face the Music

According to Paul, this is the second thing believers should do:

> So then do not be foolish, but understand what the will of the Lord is.
>
> —Ephesians 5:17

Upon first reading this, we may think it makes no sense. How can he command us to understand the Lord's will? Isn't that what we are always trying to figure out anyway?

What Paul means is this: "Don't go on willfully ignoring what you know in your heart God would have you do. Face up to it!" Paul is calling us to quit playing games; to quit excusing those things in our lives that may not be "wrong" but lead us into sin time and time again. "Quit rationalizing away those relationships that keep causing you to stumble. Only a fool continues to play games with himself!" he admonishes.

If doing business with certain individuals or groups puts you in a position that causes you to violate your convictions time and time again, quit doing business with them. If watching certain television shows causes you to lust, don't excuse them because of their entertainment value. Just quit watching them. If being with a particular group of people causes you to stumble, don't rationalize by saying, "But they are my friends." Get some new friends!

In every area of life, face up to what God would have you do. As long as you play games, as long as you ignore what you know in your heart God would have you do, you set yourself up to fail. You *camp out*, so to speak, right on the line between what is right and what is wrong. It is only a matter of time, and Satan will push you over. If you aren't willing to deal with the areas of your life that lead you into temptation, you are really not serious about dealing with temptation itself. Consistency in the Christian life demands wisdom; and wisdom demands that you face up to those things that set you up to fail.

Our Heavenly Guide

It is interesting that immediately following this passage, Paul writes,

> And do not get drunk with wine, for that is dissipation, but be filled with the Spirit.
>
> —Ephesians 5:18

The Holy Spirit plays a very important role when it comes to wisdom. If you will think back to the story of Chuck and the paralegal, you will remember that throughout the entire episode something kept warning Chuck about hiring Joyce. Chuck did not recognize it at the time, but that was the Holy Spirit working through his conscience. I call it a check in my spirit. It is hard to explain, but if you're a believer, you know exactly what I'm talking about. It's that feeling of hesitation located somewhere between your throat and your stomach. It defies logic at times. And it is usually not overbearing. It is perceived as a feeling, but it is more than a feeling.

In regard to temptation, the Holy Spirit functions much like a tour guide. Imagine that you are visiting the Grand Canyon, and you and your family sign up for a tour. What would you think if your tour guide led your entire group right up to the rail overlooking a sheer cliff and then climbed up on the narrow rail? Now imagine that as he stood there teetering back and forth, he instructed all of you to climb up for a better view!

More than likely your first response would be to call the management and have that guy locked up! Beyond that, however, your reply to his request would sound something like this, "That is quite all right. We can see just fine from back here," as you stepped back from the edge.

Do you know what the Holy Spirit wants to do for you? He wants to hold out His arms several stages away from sin and say, "This is close enough. You can see fine from here." When you ignore those warnings and move ahead, you set yourself up for disaster. You see, there is nothing harmful about balancing on the security rail overlooking the Grand Canyon. But only a fool would do such a thing. In the same respect, only a fool would continually ignore the warnings of the Holy Spirit.

A Few Steps Back

If you are serious about dealing with the temptations that harass you day after day, you may need to take a few steps back—a few wise steps toward safety and away from temptation. A friend of mine in another city had to take a few steps back in the area of lust. One afternoon we pulled up in front of a convenience store to get a paper. As I was about to get out of the car, he said, "Don't go. I'll send Sarah." Sarah was his eight-year-old daughter. He gave her some change and off she went, barely able to open the door by herself.

I made a humorous comment about his being too lazy to get the paper himself. His reply, however, explained why he sent his daughter and why he was the godly man I knew him to be. "You see," he said, "I used to go in all the time. But just inside the door to the left is a magazine rack. It is full of trashy magazines. Every time I would go in I would battle the temptation to pick one up and flip through it. I decided the wisest thing to do would be to send Sarah. That way I could avoid the temptation altogether."

Now that's taking a few steps back. Does my friend think it is wrong to go into convenience stores? No. That is not the question at all. The question is, what is the wisest thing to do?

I have another close friend who battled with changing the television channel once something of inferior quality came on. He would sit for hours, late into the night, watching whatever was on. He had to take a few steps back. He made it a rule never to turn on the television and just flip through the channels to see what was on. He always checks first to see if there is anything on worth watching. He learned that it is easier to walk away from the programming guide than from an actual show.

As we close, let me share my conviction concerning this principle. I believe this principle alone could eliminate some of the most difficult temptations confronting you. You say, "But you don't even know me." That may be true. But the people with whom I have shared this principle, and who have taken it seriously, always see a dramatic decrease in the power of the temptations with which they struggle.

Leaving the Danger Zones

Let me warn you. It may be a simple principle, but it is not always an easy one to apply. People will not understand why you can no longer go with them to the places you used to go. Even some of your Christian friends will not understand. They will think you are being legalistic or "holier than thou." Your lost friends certainly will not understand. Their comments may sting. "He can't go. He's a Christian." You may find yourself sitting at home more often.

But let me ask you again, are you really serious about gaining victory over temptation? If you are, are you willing to take a few steps back? Are you ready to step back away from the edge as if to say, "That's OK. I can see fine from here"? Are you willing to evaluate every opportunity in light of your past experiences, your present state of mind, and your future goals, plans, and dreams? Are you willing to question every invitation and decision in light of what is the "wisest" thing to do?

Are you willing to use your spare time carefully? Not always reaching for the radio or the television or the newspaper. And are you willing to face up to what you know in your heart God wants from your life? If you are, why don't you take a few minutes right now and think through those areas in which you feel you need to take a step or two back. Write them down. Perhaps you'll want to take an index card and record some of the key points of this chapter and put it in a prominent place so that you'll see it often. Then pray and ask God to forgive you for ignoring the promptings of the Holy Spirit. Ask Him to increase your sensitivity to His Spirit as He leads you down the path of wisdom and away from the danger zones.

CHAPTER 9

Dressing for the Battle

IN RECENT YEARS Americans have become more and more fashion conscious. People spend outlandish sums of money updating their wardrobes every season. Advertisers are focusing on smaller segments of the population and designing the right "look" for every age group. You can even buy designer clothes for babies, and I'm sure the babies appreciate it!

The Bible, however, speaks of a different kind of wardrobe, one that is usually overlooked by most believers. Yet it is far more important than the current style. Paul described this spiritual outfit:

Therefore, take up the full armor of God, that you may be able to resist in the evil day, and having done everything, to stand firm. Stand firm therefore, having girded your loins with truth, and having put on the breastplate of righteousness, and having shod your feet with the preparation of the gospel of peace; in addition to all, taking up the shield of faith with which you will be able to extinguish all the flaming missiles of the evil one. And take the helmet of salvation, and the sword of the Spirit, which is the word of God.

—Ephesians 6:13–17

115

No doubt you have heard sermons on the armor of God before. This is a very popular passage among preachers. But as familiar as most Christians are with the content of this passage, I find very few who take seriously Paul's application of these verses. Paul did not say, "Understand the full armor of God." Neither did he say, "Research each piece of Roman armor alluded to in these verses." Paul said, "PUT IT ON!"

Dressed for Success

Of all the people in the world, American believers should be the first to understand the force of this passage. We have different clothes for every occasion, and we are careful to wear just the right thing at the appropriate time. We have clothes to work in. Clothes to relax in. Clothes to go out on the town in. Clothes to exercise in. Clothes for weddings, formals, parties, dates, bridge clubs, pool parties, hiking, swimming, and on and on it goes. Chances are you will never catch a banker at work in his bathing suit. Or a welder at work in a tux. Neither would you find the mother of a bride wearing hiking boots at her daughter's wedding. We are careful about what we wear and where we wear it.

There is one occasion, however, that we rarely think to dress for—*war*, the spiritual war in which each of us as a believer is involved. Think about it. Would a soldier go into battle without first getting dressed for it? Not a soldier with any sense who wanted to survive. Yet every day of our lives we who profess the Lord Jesus as our Savior enter a battle. And unfortunately, most of us do not take the time to dress appropriately. Then we get to the end of the day and wonder why we don't have any willpower or discipline or resistance.

In chapter 2 we focused on the context for the temptations we experience. We saw how each temptation is a small part of an ongoing struggle between God and His enemy, the devil. We talked about how easy it is to forget that we are in a war; we are lulled into thinking that we struggle in a vacuum. And we saw how that was not the case at all. Yet even since you read that chapter, I imagine the truth about the war in which we are involved has faded from your thinking. Not intentionally, I might add. We are just not used to thinking in those terms.

Home Sweet Home

Imagine a soldier who falls asleep one night and dreams that the war is over and he is back in the States. His dream is so real that when he wakes up, he really believes he is back home and the war is over. How do you think he would dress? Like he was going into battle? I doubt it. Worse yet, what would happen to him if his squad was attacked?

Most believers do not take seriously Paul's commands in this familiar passage because we do not live conscious of the fact that we are in a war! Until we accept this simple truth, we will never develop the habit of preparing ourselves properly. Ephesians 6 is not the only passage that refers to believers being involved in a war. Paul reminded Timothy of the same truth when he said,

> Suffer hardship with me, as a good soldier of Christ Jesus. No soldier in active service entangles himself in the affairs of everyday life, so that he may please the one who enlisted him as a soldier.
>
> —2 Timothy 2:3–4

The Scriptures are clear. When we trust Christ as our Savior, we enter a war. And just like an unprepared soldier can expect to suffer in a physical war, an unprepared soldier will suffer in a spiritual war as well.

Perhaps one reason you cannot overcome temptation in your life is that you are going into battle unprepared for what you will face. Once the enemy has begun his attack, it is usually too late to start getting ready. Yet, more often than not, that is exactly when you find yourself scrambling around, looking for verses, praying meaningless prayers, and wondering why you never get anywhere.

Meet Your Opponent

Before we get into how we are to prepare for battle, we need to deal with one other matter. One of the enemy's most effective tricks is to divert the focus of our attention away from him and onto someone or something else. He wants us to see someone else as the enemy, not him. He wants husbands to see their wives as the enemy; kids to see their parents as the enemy; pastors to see their deacons or elders as the enemy.

Paul says, however, that this war is not against flesh and blood. We are not struggling with one another. Our enemy is spiritual in nature.

> For our struggle is not against flesh and blood, but against the rulers, against the powers, against the world forces of this darkness, against the spiritual forces of wickedness in the heavenly places.
>
> —Ephesians 6:12

One reason we struggle so in our earthly relationships is that we forget oftentimes where the real problem lies. That is why couples who pray together generally stay together. Prayer is the best reminder of who the enemy really is or is not! I have found in my own experience, for example, that the more our deacons pray together, the less time we spend in meetings.

Our enemy is invisible, but he is very real. He is not omniscient; he does not know everything. But he has been around long enough to have figured out our every move. He does not announce his presence with a trumpet fanfare; he is subtle. He does not attack us like the British in the Revolutionary War, wearing bright colors and making himself known. He attacks more like the colonists. He blends in well with the surroundings and waits for just the right moment.

Last of all, our enemy does not fight alone. He has under his authority scores of demonic hosts that are loose and active in the world today. There was a time when people laughed at the idea of demons and demonic possession. But more and more the truth is coming out into the open. This is especially true in countries where black magic is practiced openly. But even in our country the authorities are continually uncovering evidence of spirit worship and witchcraft.

The point is, our enemy is not alone. For the most part, overt demonic activity, such as spells and possessions, is not our concern. I do believe, however, that we struggle with demonic influence. I am no expert in the area of demons and how they work. The Scripture does not give us much insight here. But the Scripture is clear about how to deal with these hellish hosts:

> Put on the full armor of God, that you may be able to stand firm against the schemes of the devil.
> —Ephesians 6:11

Take a Chance

Before you read any further, I want you to make yourself a promise. Promise yourself that you will at least try what I am about to suggest. And not just for one day, but for seven days, one whole week. Wait! Don't keep reading until you make yourself that promise. Why? Because this is going to sound silly to some of you, especially those of you who are the more "serious" type. You know who you are. Anyway, if you will give this a try, I guarantee you won't be sorry. And if you think this is a ridiculous idea, I challenge you to study this passage on your own and figure out what you think Paul is talking about when he says, "Put on the full armor of God." I would be happy to hear from you and get your opinion.

A Closer Look

Now, at the risk of sounding contradictory, I want to take a quick look at the actual Roman armor Paul had in mind and its relationship to the spiritual armor we are to wear. The first piece he mentions is the belt: ". . . having girded your loins with truth." The Roman soldier had a girdle to put around himself. It was more like an apron than a belt. It was made of thick leather and covered his abdominal region. It also supported his sword.

The truth about God and about us as His children serves as the foundation for everything else we do as believers. That is why Paul associated the girdle with truth. The power of God is greater than the power of sin or Satan. This is the truth that gives us hope when we face temptation. The truth about us, as we have seen, is that we have been baptized into Christ. Therefore, we have been identified with His death and are dead to sin. These truths serve as the foundation for the rest of our spiritual armor.

Next Paul mentions the breastplate: ". . . and having put on the breastplate of righteousness." The breastplate was usually made of leather, although some of them were covered with metal. The breastplate protected the chest region and, thus, all the vital organs.

In ancient days, men believed the emotions resided somewhere in a person's chest. This belief probably arose from the fact that so much of what we feel emotionally is felt in that area of the body. The breastplate is associated with righteousness because what is right often conflicts with the way we feel. The breastplate of righteousness is to guard us from making decisions based on what we feel rather than what we know to be right. So often temptation begins with our emotions. We must keep our emotions in check. Not that there is anything wrong with being emotional. On the contrary, our emotions are just as much a gift of God as any part of our makeup. They were never intended, however, to be our guide.

Paul moves on to the foot covering: ". . . and having shod your feet with the preparation of the gospel of peace." The foot covering of the Roman soldier was a thick leather sandal. It wrapped around both the foot and the ankle. Sometimes the bottom was covered with spikes or nails to allow him to keep his footing in hand-to-hand combat.

The shoe is associated with peace because that is what we are to leave everywhere we go, much like a footprint. Wherever we go, we should be sharing the good news of how men and women can have peace with God.

The focus shifts here from actual clothing to a defensive weapon, the shield: ". . . in addition to all, taking up the shield of faith with which you will be able to extinguish all the flaming missiles of the evil one." The shield Paul is referring to here is not the little round shield like you see on television; it was much larger. The word translated "shield" comes from the word that meant "door." In fact, some of these shields were almost as big as doors.

They had an iron frame with thick leather stretched over it, and some of them had metal on the front. A soldier could kneel down behind such a shield and be completely protected in the front. On occasion, the Romans would soak their shields in water so that when the enemy shot flaming arrows, they were extinguished on impact.

Faith is associated with the shield because God may ask us to go places or say things that leave us open to criticism or possible failure. In and of ourselves we would be fools to even try. When we choose to obey, we walk by faith. We move out expecting God to come through for us in the areas we know we are incapable of handling. Faith, then, is our defense against fear, insecurity, anxiety, and anything else that would keep us from moving out in obedience to God.

Next Paul refers to the helmet: "And take the helmet of salvation." The helmet was the most costly and most ornate piece of the soldier's armor. It was designed to protect the entire head.

I think two ideas are implied here. First, the helmet was the piece of armor that attracted the most attention because of its elaborate design. In the same way our eternal salvation is the thing about us that should get people's attention. It is the thing for which we are to be most grateful. Jesus made that clear in Luke 10:20 ("Nevertheless do not rejoice in this, that the spirits are subject to you, but rejoice that your names are recorded in heaven").

A second idea implied in this parallel has to do with the mind. The mind is where most of our battles are won or lost. That is where the ultimate decision is made as to whether or not we will obey. We are saved from temptation when we choose with our minds to be obedient. Just as the helmet protected the head of the soldier, so our salvation gives us the potential to say yes to God and no to sin. In so doing, we are saved in a temporal sense from the act and consequences of sin.

Last of all, Paul refers to the primary offensive weapon of the Roman soldier, the sword: ". . . and the sword of the Spirit, which is the word of God." The Roman sword was designed for close combat. It was actually more of a dagger than what we normally think about when we think about a sword.

The Word of God is viewed as a sword because of its power to overcome the onslaught of the enemy. In the next chapter we will discuss exactly how this works. Suffice it to say that the Word of God sends Satan and his hosts running for cover.

A Roman soldier would not dream of going into battle without every piece of equipment secured and ready for action. To have done so would have meant certain death. Paul, understanding the day in which he lived, knew that the Ephesian believers dared not enter into the spiritual war they were involved in every day without being equally prepared.

Preparing for War

Now here is the part you may be "tempted" to skip. I have made it a habit of putting on the armor of God every morning before I get out of bed. Right over my pajamas! Remember, this is spiritual armor. Therefore, it must be put on by faith. Paul understood that spiritual warfare was somewhat of a difficult concept to grasp. So he gave us an illustration through his description of the Roman soldier. Using that mental image as a guide, we can properly prepare ourselves for the battle. But it is done by faith, not by sight.

The best way to explain this is to simply walk you through the routine I follow every morning. You do not have to do it just like I do. Paul did not leave us directions as to how to put it on by faith. There is no right or wrong way. He simply said, "Put it on."

Each morning when I first awaken I say something like this,

Good morning, Lord. Thank You for assuring me of victory today if I will but follow Your battle plan. So by faith I claim victory over _____ (I normally list some things I know I will be faced with that day).

To prepare myself for the battle ahead, by faith I put on the belt of truth. The truth about You, Lord—that You are a sovereign God who knows everything about me, both my strengths and my weaknesses. Lord, You know my breaking point and have promised not to allow me to be tempted beyond what I am able to bear. The truth about me, Lord, is that I am a new creature in

Christ and have been set free from the power of sin. I am indwelt with the Holy Spirit who will guide me and warn me when danger is near. I am Your child, and nothing can separate me from Your love. The truth is that You have a purpose for me this day—someone to encourage, someone to share with, someone to love.

Next, Lord, I want to, by faith, put on the breastplate of righteousness. Through this I guard my heart and my emotions. I will not allow my heart to attach itself to anything that is impure. I will not allow my emotions to rule in my decisions. I will set them on what is right and good and just. I will live today by what is true, not by what I feel.

Lord, this morning I put on the sandals of the gospel of peace. I am available to You, Lord. Send me where You will. Guide me to those who need encouragement or physical help of some kind. Use me to solve conflicts wherever they may arise. Make me a calming presence in every circumstance in which You place me. I will not be hurried or rushed, for my schedule is in Your hands. I will not leave a trail of tension and apprehension. I will leave tracks of peace and stability everywhere I go.

I now take up the shield of faith, Lord. My faith is in You and You alone. Apart from You, I can do nothing. With you, I can do all things. No temptation that comes my way can penetrate Your protecting hand. I will not be afraid, for You are going with me throughout this day. When I am tempted, I will claim my victory out loud ahead of time, for You have promised victory to those who walk in obedience to Your Word. So by faith I claim victory even now because I know there are fiery darts headed my way even as I pray. Lord, You already know what they are and have already provided the way of escape.

Lord, by faith I am putting on the helmet of salvation. You know how Satan bombards my mind day and night with evil thoughts, doubt, and fear. I put on this helmet that will protect my mind. I may feel the impact of his attacks, but nothing can penetrate this helmet. I choose to stop every impure and negative thought at the door of my mind. And with the helmet of salvation those thoughts will get no further. I elect to take every thought captive; I will dwell on nothing but what is good and right and pleasing to You.

Last, I take up the sword of the Spirit, which is Your Word. Thank You for the precious gift of Your Word. It is strong and powerful and able to defeat even the strongest of Satan's onslaughts. Your Word says that I am not under obligation to the flesh to obey its lusts. Your Word says that I am free from the power of sin. Your Word says that He that is in me is greater than he that is in the world. So by faith I take up the strong and powerful sword of the Spirit, which is able to defend me in time of attack, comfort me in time of sorrow, teach me in time of meditation, and prevail against the power of the enemy on behalf of others who need the truth to set them free.

So, Lord, I go now rejoicing that You have chosen me to represent You to this lost and dying world. May others see Jesus in me, and may Satan and his hosts shudder as Your power is made manifest in me. In Jesus' name I pray—AMEN.

Now, let me ask you a question. Can you think of any better way to start your day? Some might respond, "You're just psyching yourself up." To which I say, "Exactly." But I am not psyching myself up by telling myself a bunch of lies so I will like myself more or have more self-confidence. It is not self-confidence we are after; it is Christ confidence, confidence in Christ and His power through us. Sure, it sounds like a one-person pep rally, but it's all true! And we are to set our minds and emotions on what is true.

My way may not be for everybody. I even debated on whether or not to include this chapter in the book. But I want you to be victorious in your life. And apart from putting on the entire armor of God, you don't have a chance. None of us do.

Faith is being able to visualize ahead of time what God is going to do. By lying there in bed, putting on the armor piece by piece and thinking through the significance of each piece, I am exercising faith. Biblical faith. Faith in what God has done as well as what He promised to do.

First Things First

Sunday is such a busy day for me that I often stay at church all day. When I plan to do so, I always carry clothes for the service that night. More times than I care to remember I have forgotten something, either socks, a tie, or a fresh shirt. Fortunately, I have a wonderful wife who always comes to my rescue. I'll call her up, and she'll arrive a little early to guarantee that I have what I need.

I can't imagine going out to preach without having my socks on. Neither could I imagine preaching without wearing a shirt or shoes. Yet I have learned that I can get by much better without certain physical garments than I can the spiritual ones God has made available.

Paul did not suggest that we put on the whole armor of God. He *commanded* that we do so. Think for just a moment. Have you ever thought through the armor in the way I have just explained it? Have you ever taken this command seriously? Or has it always been simply an interesting passage to study and hear sermons about?

A recurring plot in war novels as well as recent science fiction movies has been that of the supposedly impregnable military complex or battleship. As the story moves toward its climax, someone discovers the Achilles' heel, the one weak spot in the defense system of the base or ship. Everyone then goes to work on a plan to capitalize on the weakness.

That was the plot of *Star Wars*, the first film in the popular trilogy about the conflict between a group of young heroes and the evil Empire. No one who has seen that movie will forget those last few scenes of the fighters shooting their way down the channel leading to the one spot where a well-placed rocket could destroy the entire base. Remember the panic on the inside of the Empire's ship when they discovered that they were vulnerable? By then, it was too late for them to do anything to save themselves.

Satan is scheming against each of us. Part of that scheme is to discover our area of least resistance. That area in which we have let down our guard. The one spot that if attacked at just the right time will put us into a spiritual tailspin. Can we really afford to move out in the mornings without first suiting up? Are we not fools to think that we are so together that we can handle Satan and his host without putting on all that armor?

I know what you are thinking. *That will take all morning*. No, it won't. You'll be surprised at how quickly it goes by. You may think, *Well, I have my quiet time at night*. I am not talking about your quiet time. Besides, whoever heard of putting on armor after the battle? Your battles begin the moment you wake up each morning. That is when you need to put on the armor.

Once again, are you willing to try this for seven days? When I first challenged my congregation with this concept, I had no idea how many of them would take me seriously. Almost immediately I received reports about the difference it made. I still get letters from people who heard that message on tape and have started suiting up for battle every morning before they start their day. If you are serious about gaining lasting victory over temptation in your life, "Put on the full armor of God, that you may be able to stand firm against the schemes of the devil." It worked for Paul. It has worked for me. I am confident it will make a difference in your life as well.

CHAPTER·10

Wielding the Sword

MY FAVORITE HOBBY is photography. An ideal vacation to me is loading up all my camera equipment and taking off for a couple of weeks on a photographic safari. I have had the joy of taking photographs all over the United States and in many foreign countries. In my endeavor to increase my skill as a photographer I have learned some important lessons. One of them is that there are no problems unique to me. Regardless of the questions I have or the predicaments I find myself in, some other photographer has already wrestled with the same dilemma and usually has discovered a solution. Until I realized this, I would let the simplest things hold me up for weeks and sometimes months.

I will never forget my first attempts at developing color film. What a disaster! I went through boxes of paper with very little to show for my hours of labor; and even at that, nothing I could be proud of. Then I met a guy who had been working in a color lab for years. He came over, showed me what I was doing wrong, and in a couple of hours we were turning out some nice pictures.

From that point on, I began to research my questions to discover how the pros dealt with them. Doing so saved me hours of headaches and freed me to do what I like best—taking photographs.

What Did Jesus Do?

Now, let's apply that same kind of thinking to this matter of temptation. First of all, let's state the problem: How do we resist temptation? Second, who has struggled with the same problem and dealt with it successfully as well as consistently? The writer of Hebrews answers that question for us,

> For we do not have a high priest who cannot sympathize with our weaknesses, but One who has been tempted in all things as we are, yet without sin.
>   —Hebrews 4:15

If Jesus is "the pro," then we would do well to study His strategy for dealing with temptation. Strangely enough, Jesus' approach is so straightforward and simple that many believers tend to overlook it entirely. Others, after hearing it, make the most ridiculous excuses as to why they cannot follow His example. In doing so, however, they resign themselves to a life of defeat.

Unfortunately, we have only one clear passage of Scripture describing Christ's encounter with temptation. We know from the Hebrews passage cited above that He was tempted more often than this, but the Holy Spirit chose not to include these in the Gospels.

The Ultimate Temptation

Matthew sets the stage for us in the first two verses of this narrative,

> Then Jesus was led up by the Spirit into the wilderness to be tempted by the devil. And after He had fasted forty days and forty nights, He then became hungry.
>   —Matthew 4:1–2

This last phrase may be the greatest understatement of all time: "He then became hungry." I think starving would be more like it! The text seems to indicate that Christ was unaware of His physical needs during this time. G. Campbell Morgan made this comment about this period in Christ's life,

> Notice carefully that it was after the lapse of forty days that Jesus was hungry. It would seem as though during their passing, He was unconscious of His physical need. His thoughts had been of things within the spiritual realm, and the demands of the physical had been unrecognized. At the close of the forty days the sense of need swept over Him. He was hungry.
>
> —*The Crisis of the Christ*, p. 165

Now before we go rushing into the rest of the story, let's pause for a moment and think. Forty days without food. One month and ten days. It is difficult for some of us to go one hour and ten minutes. No doubt the reason for choosing to include this particular temptation scenario in the Scripture is that there was probably no other time in Christ's earthly life when He was more susceptible to temptation. He was weak physically from not having eaten. He was probably drained emotionally from His prolonged time of prayer. If there was ever a time to tempt the Lord Jesus, that was it; and Satan knew it. At the same time, if there is a way to have victory when tempted in circumstances such as these, we need to know about it. It is doubtful that we will ever find ourselves in a more vulnerable position.

"And the Tempter Came"

Matthew continues,

And the tempter came and said to Him, "If You are the Son of God, command that these stones become bread." But He answered and said, "It is written, 'Man shall not live on bread alone, but on every word that proceeds out of the mouth of God.'"

—Matthew 4:3–4

Thus ended round one. But the devil didn't give up.

Then the devil took Him into the holy city; and he had Him stand on the pinnacle of the temple, and said to Him, "If You are the Son of God throw Yourself down; for it is written, 'He will give His angels charge concerning You'; and 'On their hands they will bear You up, lest You strike Your foot against a stone.'" Jesus said to him, "On the other hand, it is written, 'You shall not put the Lord your God to the test.'"

—Matthew 4:5–7

And so ended round two.

Again, the devil took Him to a very high mountain, and showed Him all the kingdoms of the world, and their glory; and he said to Him, "All these things will I give You, if You fall down and worship me." Then Jesus said to him, "Begone, Satan! For it is written, 'You shall worship the Lord your God, and serve Him only.'" Then the devil left Him; and behold, angels came and began to minister to Him.

—Matthew 4:8–11

This is hard for me to comprehend. The Son of God—the One who knows all things and has the power to do all things, the One whose words we study, memorize, and meditate on—never made an original comment during the entire interaction.

He did not say, "What do you mean *if* I am the Son of God? Of course I am." He never drew on His own wit. He never even relied on His own power. He simply responded with the truth of His Father's Word. That was all it took. Nothing creative. Nothing fancy. Just the plain truth directed at the deception behind each of Satan's requests.

The lesson is unmistakably clear. If the only One who ever lived a sinless life combated temptation with God's Word, how do we hope to survive without it? I am so glad He did outsmart Satan in a battle of the minds. I have tried that and failed miserably. I am glad He did not discuss the temptation with Satan and resist him that way. Eve tried that, and she got nowhere. I am glad Jesus did not use raw willpower, though I imagine He could have. My willpower is pretty useless when Satan really turns on the steam. Jesus verbally confronted Satan with the truth; and eventually Satan gave up and left.

The Power of the Word

There are four primary reasons that a well-chosen passage or verse of Scripture is so effective against temptation. First of all, God's Word exposes the sinfulness of whatever you are being tempted to do. This is extremely important because one of Satan's subtle snares is to convince you that what you are being tempted to do is really not so bad after all. What is wrong with turning a stone into bread if you are hungry and have the power to do so? There is no law against that. What is wrong with a little sex? You love her, don't you? There is nothing wrong with leaving that income off your tax form; the government takes too much of your money as it is.

Satan has such a smooth way of rationalizing sin. Once you bring a temptation under the scrutiny of God's Word, you expose it for what it is—a lie. The lie behind Satan's first request of Jesus was, "Jesus, You have the right to meet Your God-given needs when You deem appropriate. You're hungry now, so eat!" Satan was tempting Jesus to take things into His own hands on the basis of His personal needs. Jesus' response brought to light the motive behind Satan's request. In essence He said, "My ultimate responsibility is not simply to satisfy My physical needs, but to obey My Father in heaven." The truth of His Father's Word showed the sinfulness of Satan's request.

So often the things you are tempted with seem so harmless. It is not until you shine the truth of God's Word on those temptations that you see what is really at stake. God's Word takes you right to the heart of the matter. It allows you to see things for what they really are.

Divine Perspective

A second reason the Word of God is so effective against temptation is that you gain God's viewpoint through it. The Scripture provides you with a divine perspective on the temptation you are facing as well as your relationship to it.

Since many temptations carry a strong emotional punch, you tend to get caught up in your feelings. You perceive the temptation as something that is a part of you rather than something happening to you. Once you identify with the feelings temptation evokes, it becomes increasingly difficult to respond correctly. The truth of Scripture allows you to be more objective about the temptations you face. God's Word enables you to see temptation for what it is. It allows you to separate yourself just far enough mentally so that you can deal with it successfully.

The Displacement Principle

Another reason for turning to God's Word in times of temptation is what one pastor calls the principle of displacement (Bud Palmberg, "Private Sins of Public Ministry," *Leadership* magazine [Winter 1988]: 23). This principle is based on the premise that it is impossible *not* to think of something. For example, stop reading for a moment and try your best not to think about pink elephants. It is impossible. You cannot avoid thinking about something. What you must do is focus your attention somewhere else when your thoughts are dominated by a seductive topic.

It is clear that the sinful thoughts accompanying temptation must be redirected, and when you turn your attention to the Word of God during temptation, you do just that. No doubt Paul had this in mind when he wrote,

> Finally, brethren, whatever is true, whatever is honorable, whatever is right, whatever is pure, whatever is lovely, whatever is of good repute, if there is any excellence and if anything worthy of praise, let your mind dwell on these things.
>
> —Philippians 4:8

He echoed the same idea in Colossians when he said,

> Set your mind on the things above, not on the things that are on earth.
>
> —Colossians 3:2

If you don't shift your attention away from the temptation, you may begin some form of mental dialogue: *I really shouldn't. But I haven't done this in a long time. I am really going to hate myself later. Why not? I've already blown it anyway. I'll do it just this once, and tomorrow I'll start over.* When you allow these little discussions to begin, you are sunk. The longer you talk, the more time the temptation has to settle into your emotions and will.

You are to use the Word of God to head temptation off at the pass. As soon as the thought enters your mind, you are to turn your thoughts in the direction of God's Word. Eve's biggest mistake was talking things over with Satan.

She should have repeated back to him verbatim what God had commanded her to do and then just walked away. Instead she got into a discussion.

Faith

The fourth reason the Word of God is so effective against temptation is that you are expressing faith when you turn your attention to His Word. You are saying, "I believe God is able to get me through this; I believe He is mightier than the power of sin, my flesh, and Satan himself." Nothing moves God like the active faith of His people.

Building an Arsenal

Most believers would find the above discussion very convincing—and probably not very original. The account of Jesus' temptation is convincing in itself without any commentary. So why, then, do so many Christians continue to complain about their inability to deal with temptation and at the same time excuse their ignorance of God's Word? "I don't understand it. I can't memorize Scripture. I don't have time."
.
There are no good excuses. It really comes down to one thing: laziness. We are just too lazy to fill the arsenal of our minds with those truths we need to combat the lies of the enemy. And consequently, when he attacks, we get wiped out.

So many books, seminars, and study courses are available on how to understand the Bible that it would take a lifetime to get through them all. And yet most believers refuse to take the time to remedy their ignorance.

My son, Andy, works with the young people of our church. Every year he goes through a course designed to teach the teenagers how to have an effective quiet time. Part of that training covers Scripture memorization and meditation. Every year he hears the same excuse, "I can't understand the Bible." Here is how he answers that excuse:

> Imagine that tomorrow the best-looking girl in your school (or a guy if he's talking to girls) walks up to you and says, "Hey, I've been watching you, and I think you're cute. I would love for you to come over to my house for dinner tomorrow night. Here is a map. I'll see you around 7:00." As she walks away, you can't believe it. It's too good to be true. You race over to your locker and open the map to see where she lives. It's the messiest thing you've ever seen in your life. You can't tell which way is up. How many of you guys would say, "Too bad, I can't understand the map. I guess I won't go"? How many of you would do whatever you had to in order to figure out what the map meant?

At that point all the hands in the group usually go up.

> Why would we go to great lengths to figure out a map to a girl's house, but when it comes to the Word of God, we read a few verses and give up the moment we don't understand something?

The point of his illustration is simple. We do what we want to do. After we have been convinced of the importance of a task, we can usually figure out a way to get it done. Our problem with learning about the Word of God is not time, knowledge, or education; it is a problem with priorities.

I know Christians who spend hours figuring out crossword puzzles, but they declare they don't have time to study the Word of God. Let's get real practical. If you spend two hours a day watching television and ten minutes each day reading God's Word, which do you think is going to have a greater overall impact on your life?

Jesus had the truth He needed fresh in His mind. It

was only one thought away. He didn't struggle to dig up some long-forgotten memory verse from primaries. "Now hold on a minute. I memorized a verse about that one time. Let's see, it went something like . . ." Sound familiar?

To effectively combat the onslaughts of the enemy, you need an arsenal of verses on the tip of your tongue. Verses that are so familiar that they come to your mind without any conscious effort on your part. If you have to dig them up from the caverns of your memory, they will do you no good. There isn't time for that in the midst of temptation.

Truths for Lies

The process of Scripture memorization is never easy, but most things in life worth having cost something. A few pointers will make it easier for you, though. First of all, select verses that focus on the areas in which you are most tempted. At the end of this chapter I have listed some categories of temptation along with some corresponding passages of Scripture.

Every man, for instance, should have several verses on the tip of his tongue that have to do with lust or immorality. We are bombarded at every turn with the promise of pleasure through illicit sex. What a lie! Yet all of us have the potential to buy into that way of thinking and thus fall.

All of us should have a verse on hand for gossip. It's so easy to participate in pointless chatter about other people. As soon as you hear someone begin or as soon as a juicy tidbit comes to your mind concerning someone else, you should be reminded that "if anyone thinks himself to be religious, and yet does not bridle his tongue but deceives his own heart, this man's [or woman's] religion is worthless" (James 1:26). It should be that natural.

We all need a verse to remind us of our Christian duty to obey the laws set forth by our government. When we are tempted to break them, we need to be reminded that it is God's will for us to "submit [yourselves] for the Lord's sake to every human institution. . . . For such is the will of God that by doing right [we] may silence the ignorance of foolish men" (1 Pet. 2:13–15).

Do you know why God wants us to obey the law? It's not because they are all good laws. We are to keep the law for testimony's sake. To do otherwise is to be hypocritical. Once again, the truth of God's Word exposes the lie of Satan. He says, "Go ahead and break the law. Everybody else does. It's a dumb law anyway. Besides, doesn't the Bible say something about being free from the Law?" But Satan's arguments collapse under the scrutiny of God's Word.

Keep It Simple

Another thing to keep in mind when memorizing Scripture is to keep it simple. Set small goals at first. One verse a week is enough to begin with. Often after reading a book on Scripture memorization or hearing someone's testimony concerning it, we set out with the intention of memorizing the entire New Testament. After about four verses, we become discouraged and give up altogether.

Remember the purpose in all of this. Memorizing Scripture isn't the ultimate goal. It is just a means to an end. The reason to memorize Scripture is to provide you with an arsenal to use the next time Satan attacks.

Howard Hendricks tells a humorous story about a kid in his church who had memorized the entire New Testament. He could quote the text and he knew the references as well. Hendricks says you could say to this kid, "Ephesians 4:9," and he would start right there and keep right on going.

During the course of time, someone began noticing that money was missing from the offering collected in the junior boys' class. Sure enough, the adults discovered that this same kid who knew half the Bible was stealing money from the plate. Dr. Hendricks was given the responsibility of confronting him.

In a sincere attempt to handle things in a biblical manner, he sat down with the boy and said, "You know the Bible says . . . ," and he quoted a verse on stealing. Quickly, the boy looked up at Dr. Hendricks and informed him he had misquoted the verse! As the conversation ensued, it became apparent that the youngster was oblivious to the connection between what the Scripture said and his action of taking money from the offering plate. All that is to say, memorizing Scripture isn't enough. It is simply one in a series of stages. The ultimate goal is to have the truth ready at a moment's notice.

Review, Review, Review

The only way to keep something fresh and to guarantee that it has become part of your long-term memory is to review it. The simplest way I know to develop a review system is to use index cards. That way you can keep all your verses together. When you have a few minutes between appointments or tasks, you can pull them out and review them.

Several companies sell Scripture memorization programs. Some of these have a review system built in. What you will find, however, is that the verses corresponding with the temptations you face will stick most readily in your mind. I have claimed some verses so many times that I can quote them without even concentrating. These are the ones I rely on every day. For the verses that you don't use as often, you need a review system.

Think about it this way. If you memorize one verse a week for a year, and even skip two weeks for vacation, that is fifty verses. That is more verses than many Christians learn in a lifetime. Just think about how far along you would be if you had started last year at this time. If you don't begin now, next year you will look back and wish you had.

A Personal Matter

Another thing I would suggest is to personalize the Scripture you memorize. The first time I heard about this idea was at a Basic Youth Conflicts Seminar. Bill Gothard shared a personal testimony about the difference this made in his spiritual life. That was over fifteen years ago, and I've been doing it ever since then.

Personalizing Scripture makes it come alive. Substitute your name or a personal pronoun for pronouns such as *you* and *we*. "Thank You, Lord, that I am not under obligation to my flesh to obey the lust thereof." "Lord, I choose to set my mind on the things above and not on the things on earth, for I have died and my life is hidden with Christ in God.""Lord, I am casting all my cares on You, for I know You care for me."

"Call Upon the Name of the Lord"

One last suggestion is to get in the habit of quoting these verses audibly when you are tempted. This may seem a little strange at first, but there are good reasons to do this. First, I do not believe Satan and his host can read our minds. He can put thoughts there, but the Scripture does not indicate that he can read them.

If that is true, simply thinking through a verse poses the enemy no threat. It may help you refocus your attention and therefore relieve the pressure for a time. But in terms of really challenging the devil and putting him in his place, I am not convinced that mentally reviewing Scripture does much good.

The second reason speaking the truth aloud is important is that it shifts the point of tension from an internal conflict to an external one. Throughout this book, I have referred to our tendency to emotionally latch on to temptation and own it as part of our being, to mistakenly think, *This is the way I am. Otherwise why would I feel this way?*

When you speak the truth out loud, you are reminded that *you* are not your enemy. And He that is within you is not your enemy. Your enemy is the devil. He roams around like a lion looking for someone to devour (1 Pet. 5:8). Satan hates to be recognized. He would much rather have you internalize the battle so that he can remain anonymous.

There are times when we are our own worst enemy. This is certainly the case when we ignore the principle outlined in chapter 8 and make unwise decisions. But even in those cases, I have found it extremely helpful to speak the truth aloud.

Now I'm not talking about shouting it at the top of your lungs. There are times when you will simply have to whisper it. At other times you can speak in a normal tone of voice. You may feel silly the first time you do this, but you will notice an immediate difference when you do.

When you speak the truth out loud, it is as if you have taken a stand with God against the enemy. When I begin speaking the truth aloud, I often feel a sense of courage and conviction sweeping over me. Usually this turns into joy, and what started out as a bad thing becomes a time of praise and rejoicing. If you don't believe me, just try it.

The last reason I think it is a good idea to speak aloud when tempted is that Jesus did it. Need I say more?

Conformed or Transformed?

When you get involved in building up an arsenal of verses, you will be in the process of doing something else as well—renewing your mind. To renew something is a two-stage process. It involves removing the old and putting on the new. When you fill your mind with the truth of God's

Word so that you can root out the error that keeps you from being victorious, you are renewing your mind.

The importance of this process cannot be overemphasized. It guards you against falling prey to temptation and it protects you from being brainwashed by the world. This is what Paul was talking about when he wrote,

> And do not be conformed to this world, but be transformed by the renewing of your mind, that you may prove what the will of God is, that which is good and acceptable and perfect.
>
> —Romans 12:2

The "how to" of defending ourselves against becoming like the world is to renew our minds. Everywhere we turn we find ourselves being asked to adopt a way of thinking that is contrary to what Christ and His church stand for. Unless you and I make some effort to combat this onslaught of propaganda, we will fall victim to its debilitating poison.

Get Started!

I hope you will not wait until you have finished reading this book to start developing your arsenal. That is what Satan would have you do. Why? He wants you to forget. I have listed several categories of things most of us struggle with, and I have included a few verses to get you started. Begin with the area that troubles you the most. Then work on other areas. Don't start too fast. Don't give up if you miss a couple of weeks. And above all, remember, if the perfect, sinless, sovereign Son of God relied on Scripture to pull Him through, what hope do you have without it?

Truth for Lies

Any temptation that seems to be unbearable.—1 Corinthians 10:13

The temptation to gossip—James 1:26.

The temptation to lust—Psalm 119:9; Proverbs 6:24–33; Galatians 6:7–8; Colossians 3:2–3.

The temptation to fear—Psalm 56:3; John 14:1.

The temptation to think you are getting away with sin— 2 Corinthians 5:10; Galatians 6:7–8.

Troubled by circumstances—John 16:33.

The temptation to get involved with debatable things— 2 Corinthians 5:9.

The temptation not to do the wise thing—Ephesians 5:15–16.

The temptation not to obey your parents—Ephesians 6:1–3.

The temptation to disobey the law—1 Peter 2:13–15.

The temptation to demand your own way—1 Corinthians 6:19–20.

The temptation to do things that will harm your body— 1 Corinthians 6:19–20.

CHAPTER 11

No Lone Rangers

ONE OF THE great truths of the Christian faith is that each believer has the opportunity to develop a personal relationship with God through Jesus Christ. This is one of the most significant differences between Christianity and other established religions of the world. This truth, however, like any other truth, has negative potential as well when it is stressed to the point of being out of balance with the rest of God's Word.

It is true that each of us can approach God independently. He hears and answers our prayers. It is true that He can empower us to deal with the difficulties in this life and that His grace is always sufficient. But God never intended for any of us to function as spiritual lone rangers. At no point does the intimacy of our walk with God relieve us of our responsibility and accountability to the whole body of Christ. Such independence does not work in a physical body; neither will it work in the church of the Lord Jesus Christ.

The Final Stage

The final stage in developing a self-defense against temptation is *accountability*. Generally speaking, accountability is a willingness to provide an explanation of one's activities, conduct, and fulfillment of assigned responsibilities. All of us are accountable to someone in some way. On the job, you are accountable to your employer or to a board of some kind. You are expected to accomplish certain tasks in an allotted amount of time. Since your employer hired you and is paying you for your work, he has the right to hold you accountable. If he doesn't feel you are working up to par, your employer has every right in the world to confront you and demand an explanation.

Accountability of that sort is something we can all relate to in one way or another. Most of us began to learn that lesson when we started our first job. But moral and ethical accountability is something most people have thought very little about. It seems appropriate to save this particular area of defense for last, not because it is the least important, but because it is the most overlooked. And no wonder. Who wants to admit secret sins to someone? Who wants to appear weak? Who wants to invite criticism? The whole idea of providing someone with an explanation of my moral conduct seems a little strange. "That is nobody's business! That is between me and the Lord." But is it really?

We have mistakenly come to believe that since we have a personal relationship with the God who promises to help us when we are tempted, we should omit any mention of that aspect of our lives from the rest of our relationships. After all, temptation is a private thing. *Temptation may be a private thing, but sin rarely is.* Sin eventually reaches out beyond the confines of a single life and touches the lives of all those around it. Ask any woman whose husband has left her for someone else. His private temptation eventually became public knowledge. Ask the husband whose wife's private struggle with alcohol eventually became a source of embarrassment to the whole family. Ask the parents of the teenager whose private struggle with failure eventually led to suicide. And what about the countless families who lose everything because of the father's private struggle with drugs or gambling? Sure, temptation is a private matter; but sin never is.

The real question is, who is going to find out and when? "But my temptation is so small, there is no way it is going to turn into a public scandal." Just remember, every single person whose sin became public knowledge said the same thing. No one ever anticipates the harm that can come to others. Satan does everything possible to keep that thought from ever entering the mind.

Working It Out

Specifically, what we are talking about here is a relationship with a person or a small group of people in which you can share anything: your hurts, your fears, your temptations, your victories, and even your defeats. It must be a relationship committed to honesty, openness and, above all, privacy. Later in this chapter we will focus on the "how to's" of an accountability relationship, but at this point I want to explain why the concept of accountability is so effective against temptation.

Recurring temptations carry with them a great deal of emotional stress. This results from both the internal struggle and the guilt once we give in. An accountability relationship provides an outlet for those feelings and frustrations that otherwise have no other outlet. In fact, part of the deceptiveness of sin is that we feel the only way we can deal with the internal pressure we are experiencing is to go ahead and sin. Sin, however, only compounds the problem. Then we have to cope with guilt *and* the possibility of others finding out. Before long, the inner frustration builds up again anyway.

Having someone to whom we can spill our guts provides us with a temporary substitute for the frustration we feel as well as the sin we are tempted to commit. I say "temporary" because until we deal with the root issues of a problem, the pressure and frustration will eventually return. In this respect, an accountability relationship serves as a kind of halfway house.

Many times in my life I have been so frustrated with the way things were going at church or at home that I just wanted to run. In those times I have turned not only to the Lord, but to my friends as well. I tell them everything I am feeling; what I would like to do; where I would like to go. Usually by the time I am finished, I am all right again. I don't really need for them to say anything. Just knowing that they will listen with open minds and hearts is enough. Most of the time there are some things that need to be dealt with in the areas that cause me frustration. But after I pour out my heart, they seem much more manageable than before.

I believe most extramarital affairs have little or nothing to do with sex. Pressures at home and work build, and men and women feel like running away from all responsibility and accountability. At the same time everybody has a desire for intimacy. And since nothing kills intimacy like tension, the first inclination is to look for intimacy somewhere new, somewhere free of tension.

Everybody needs someone to run to, someone who will listen, pray, and offer wise counsel when appropriate. Individuals who have someone like that will find it much easier to deal with temptation, for they have an alternative.

Never the First

There is a second reason why an accountability relationship aids in the struggle with temptation. The apostle Paul hit on it when he wrote,

> No temptation has overtaken you but such as is common to man.
>
> —1 Corinthians 10:13

Regardless of what you are struggling with, you are not the first. Others have walked this road before you. And they probably wrote a book about it! The point is, your struggles are not unique. Time after time I have poured out my heart to other men expecting them to look surprised. Instead, they just smile and say, "You, too?" Knowing you are not alone relieves some of the pressure.

Couples who come to me for premarital counseling often share the struggle they are having in the area of physical intimacy. Often the guilt they feel for even having the struggle clouds their ability to deal with the problem rationally. I have learned that one of the most helpful things to do is to pair them up with a couple who have just recently been married. I encourage them to talk about the engagement period, and eventually the subject of physical intimacy surfaces. Once the newly married couple share the struggle they had in that area, the engaged couple often feel some sense of relief. Not that this gives them license to sin. It does, however, remove the false guilt they were experiencing for being tempted in the first place.

Often the experience of others can provide us with great insight into how to approach the temptations we are facing. Sometimes simply talking through a problem leads to the discovery of a solution. Anyone in a management position knows the value of brainstorming. Pooling the wisdom and creativity of a concerned group always gives birth to new ideas and solutions. When we discuss our spiritual struggles with others, the same thing occurs. Our accountability partners have the advantage of objectivity and fresh insight. They are able to bring their experience and the experience of others they know to bear on our situation.

Stubborn Love

There is one other way in which an accountability relationship can help during times of temptation. The following story illustrates it perfectly. A member of our church who was away at school at the time told me about it. I'll call him Al. It was the Thursday night of exam week, and both he and a friend of his, Randy, had taken their last exam that afternoon. They were ready to paint the town that evening. Since they were both believers, painting the town amounted to going out to eat and driving around town with the sunroof open. On the way to pick up Randy, Al stopped by the apartment next door to see if Stacy would like to go along. Stacy and Al hadn't really ever dated, but being next-door neighbors, they did see each other frequently.

Stacy was not doing anything that evening, so she decided to join the boys for an evening of harmless fun. Al and Randy were pretty wound up from having been cooped up all week studying. As the evening wore on, Randy couldn't help noticing that Stacy and Al were getting pretty cozy with each other. After a while it became obvious to Randy that they were ready to take him home so they could be alone.

As they dropped him off, Randy had an uneasy feeling about Al and Stacy. He knew Al pretty well, well enough to know that he was not acting like himself. Heading upstairs to his apartment, he grew increasingly worried about Al and Stacy. They were both believers, but they had apparently gotten caught up in the excitement of the moment.

Randy went inside and called Al on the phone. It was just as he had expected. He could hear Stacy talking in the background; Al had invited her over. "Al, this is Randy," he said. "I'm coming over to spend the night with you."

Al admitted that he had gotten mad when Randy announced he was coming over. "He didn't even ask me if he could come. He just told me to get ready!" By the time Randy showed up, Stacy was gone. Al had fixed Randy a pallet on the floor by his bed.

As Al related this story to me, he said, "We both lay there in the dark several minutes without saying a word. Finally, I said, 'Thanks.' That was all I had to say. He understood. 'No problem,' he said. 'I know you would have done the same for me.'"

Now that is accountability. Sometimes an accountability partner has to take an active role in the temptation process. We all need a friend like Randy, someone who is willing to risk criticism for the sake of our spiritual growth and moral protection. Solomon put it this way,

> Better is open rebuke
> Than love that is concealed.
> Faithful are the wounds of a friend,
> But deceitful are the kisses of an enemy.
> —Proverbs 27:5–6

Bearing One Another's Burdens

People often object to the idea of accountability because they don't feel that what other people are doing is any of their business. But just the opposite is true. The Bible says within the body of Christ we all have a responsibility to one another. Listen to what the apostle Paul said regarding this subject of accountability:

> Brethren, even if a man is caught in any trespass, you who are spiritual, restore such a one in a spirit of gentleness; each one looking to yourself, lest you too be tempted. Bear one another's burdens, and thus fulfill the law of Christ. For if anyone thinks he is something when he is nothing, he deceives himself.
> —Galatians 6:1–3

Paul said that if a believer is caught in sin, the strong members of the church are to help shoulder the responsibility of that person's sin. They are to work with the sinner and help him get back on track. The implication is that our sin is other people's business. And conversely, their sin becomes part of our business or responsibility. Sin is not just the responsibility of the people directly affected. This passage does not even mention those people. Paul said Christians who aren't even involved in what is going on are to come to the rescue of those caught in sin.

If confronting our brothers and sisters in Christ about their sin is being "nosy," Paul never would have written those verses. At the same time, if you and I were expected to work out our problems without the aid of other Christians, Paul never would have written them, either. Nowhere in Scripture are we told that our sin is something just between us and God. The Bible teaches just the opposite.

A woman in our church in Miami was married for only a short time when she found out her husband was a homosexual. Soon after she discovered it, he left her to be with his lover. As I talked with her, she said something I shall never forget. "After I was divorced, several of my friends came to me and said they knew he was gay. When I asked them why they didn't say anything to me, they said, 'We didn't think it was any of our business.'"

Her friends were dead wrong. They violated a scriptural principle. After hearing her story, I made up my mind never to stand by quietly and watch a friend make what I was sure in my heart was a mistake. This resolution has made me very unpopular with people at times. People have left my church over things I have confronted them about. But when I start thinking that maybe I should keep my mouth shut, I always remember what Solomon said,

> He who rebukes a man will
>   afterward find more favor
> Than he who flatters with the tongue.
> —Proverbs 28:23

It is amazing how through the years people have come back to me or written letters to apologize for their reaction to my warnings. More often than not, they admit that they should have listened.

Remember this, in an accountability relationship you are not responsible for how the other person responds to your warnings or counsel. You cannot guarantee that the individual will take what you say to heart. But you are responsible to tell the truth and then continue to love that person through the whole process.

You and Your Accountability Partner

The Bible doesn't outline a program for accountability groups. There are no rules that govern when and how often you should meet with your accountability partner or partners. I have seen it work in a variety of ways. My daughter, Becky, gets together with her partner once a month. In between meetings they stay in touch by phone. Andy meets with his accountability partner every week for breakfast. One pastor on our staff meets with his group on Tuesday evenings. Some of our teenagers meet during lunch at school.

Accountability partners don't necessarily have to have a formal meeting. I know two who work out together three mornings a week. They discuss things as they exercise. One fellow in our church meets his partner once a week on the golf course. I go hunting and fishing with mine on a regular basis.

An accountability partner should be someone of the same sex. And you should be naturally attracted to that person; that is, you wouldn't mind developing a lifelong friendship. The more you have in common, the better. You may have the most helpful discussions in the midst of some other activity you are participating in together.

Your accountability partner should be someone you respect spiritually. I don't mean that the person should be a Bible scholar or should have been a Christian since adolescence. Rather, your partner should be someone who is seeking to gain God's perspective on life and really wants to develop personally in keeping with God's desires. Chances are, you already know someone who would make you a good partner. It may just be a matter of discussing it together. Or you may just begin to open up and let things take their natural course.

Striking a Balance

The last thing you want is a relationship with someone who criticizes you every time you get together. But you don't want someone who will let you get by with murder, either. The key here is a balance between encouragement and exhortation or instruction, but not a fifty-fifty balance. The relationship should be about 75 percent encouragement and 25 percent exhortation.

Another way to handle this is to make an agreement to never give unsolicited advice or criticism. If you want your partner's opinion on a decision you are making, ask for it. Remember, you are not there to assume the role of therapist. You are meeting as friends who are committed to love and care for each other.

Most of the accountability partners I know did not begin their relationship with that in mind. They were just good friends who eventually felt comfortable sharing their most personal struggles with each other. The more natural it is, the better.

Why Not?

In general, women have an easier time developing accountability relationships than men do. There are several reasons for this. The biggest hindrance for men, however, is ego. God calls it pride. We want to handle things ourselves. There is no task too difficult, no mountain too high, no temptation too strong . . . , and on and on we go. You know the old saying, "Me and God is a majority." Sounds good, but it doesn't work well in real life.

The bottom line is that we don't like admitting our weaknesses to anyone else (as if those around us did not already know), especially to another man. At least with a woman there is a chance we will get sympathy and possibly a shoulder to cry on. But another guy? We think, *He will see right through me. He may make me face myself as I really am. God forbid, I may look bad!*

So you are left with a choice to make. Are you willing to expose your weaknesses to a hand-picked individual or group now, or would you rather run the risk of having your weaknesses exposed to the whole world later? We all need somebody to talk to. Don't let your pride keep you from finding somebody. The more prominent and successful you become, the more you need accountability. Unfortunately, it will become increasingly difficult to find because people may be intimidated. "Who am I to offer him advice?" they may ask. But don't give up. There may come a time in your life when your accountability partner is all that stands between you and disaster.

Starting Young

Wise parents of teenagers encourage their kids to develop relationships with godly singles or college students, people they can look up to. At that stage in their development kids often do not feel comfortable talking about private matters with their parents. But they need somebody other than their peers with whom to share. As a teenager, my daughter began meeting with a woman who is her accountability partner to this day. I'm so grateful for the people God sent our way to fill the gap for our kids while they were going through those difficult teenage years. Accountability is for everybody. The younger you can begin teaching your children this fact, the better.

No Lone Rangers

Now that I think about it, this chapter may be mistitled. Even the Lone Ranger had Tonto. We all need someone like Tonto. Someone who knows us inside out. Someone we can't deceive. Someone who will accept us as we are, yet who knows how to push us toward Christlikeness. Someone we can depend on. Such a friend is hard to find but is worth more than all the treasures of the earth. Friends of that stature may one day keep us from losing all that is dear to us.

Recently I heard in full the public confession given by one of my brothers in the ministry who had allowed his involvement with pornography to wreck his personal life and ministry. He described the measures he went to in order to be freed of his addiction: fasting, praying, crying out to God. But nothing seemed to work. Then he said something I will never forget. He said, "I realize now that if I had turned to my brothers and sisters in Christ for help, I would have been delivered."

No one is a spiritual island. We need one another. It is my prayer that you will find someone with whom you can develop an accountability relationship. Whatever you are struggling with, you are not alone. Ask God to bring into your life the kind of person Solomon had in mind when he wrote,

> A man of many friends comes to ruin,
> But there is a friend who sticks
>   closer than a brother.
> —Proverbs 18:24

PART III

DISCOVERING
THE
TRUTH

CHAPTER 12

Our Misunderstandings

IN CHAPTER 5 we discussed the fact that Satan is scheming against believers. A big part of overcoming temptation is understanding exactly what Satan is up to and how he goes about carrying out his schemes. In this chapter we are going to look at six commonly held theories regarding temptation. As we will see, none of them can be supported biblically. What's worse, these misunderstandings cause many well-meaning believers to live under a burden God never intended them to bear; their expectation level becomes totally unrealistic. Consequently, they become discouraged and unmotivated. I believe Satan is the source of these misunderstandings, for at the bottom of each is a distortion of God's truth.

In Paul's second letter to the Corinthians he pointed out that ignorance of Satan's schemes would allow Satan to take advantage of them (2 Cor. 2:11). A misunderstanding in the area of temptation does just that. It sets a person up to be taken advantage of. It is like the situation of a woman who takes an office job but never receives instruction about exactly what is expected of her. Anyone in this position is set up to be taken advantage of. As people discover her naivete, they will tend to pass off some of their undesirable duties on the "new girl." Soon she will find herself swamped with more work than she could ever finish. As the unfinished work piles up, she becomes discouraged and feels like a failure. But she isn't a failure at all! It just appears that way because she never knew exactly what was expected of her.

Perhaps part of the reason you are so discouraged is that you have heaped upon yourself unrealistic expectations, expectations God never intended for you to live with. Consequently, you are set up to be abused by Satan, maybe even to the point of giving up altogether. As we look at these six misunderstandings, examine your heart to see if either consciously or subconsciously you are operating from the basis of one or more of these falsehoods.

1. To Be Tempted Is to Sin.

Oftentimes when we are tempted, the feelings associated with that temptation are so strong that we associate the evil feelings with our character rather than with the temptation. Then we condemn ourselves for even having such feelings. Without actually giving in to the temptation we feel as if we are already guilty. That is when Satan usually chimes in, "Well, you might as well go ahead now and do it! After all, what kind of person would even come up with such an awful idea? You are already guilty."

We must keep in mind that we are not responsible for what flashes through our minds. Our responsibility is to control the things that dominate our thoughts. Paul clarified this difference to the Corinthian believers when he wrote,

> We are destroying speculations and every lofty thing raised up against the knowledge of God, and we are taking every thought captive to the obedience of Christ.
> —2 Corinthians 10:5

If God expected us to be able to control what came into our minds, why would He move the apostle Paul to instruct believers to take "every thought captive"? He implies that we cannot control what rushes into our minds. What we can and must do, however, is take control of each thought and deal with it. That is, we should dwell on the good and drive out the bad.

Our environment determines to a great extent what comes into our minds. Even the most cautious people will at some point be exposed visually and audibly to things that will summon ungodly thoughts and feelings. We cannot control what other people wear or say. We cannot control what we are invited to participate in (although we can obviously control what we choose to participate in). We cannot control what we accidentally overhear in the office or in the rest room. All of these things are thrust upon us without our consent.

Many of these external messages pack an emotional punch. And when our feelings get involved, things often become confusing. These feelings may raise serious doubts in our minds about our commitment, and for some of us, it can become a question of salvation. "If I was really committed, would I feel this way?" "Would a real Christian want to do that?"

These feelings are usually natural, God-given feelings. The problem is that when we are tempted, our feelings are being focused outside the parameters God has established for us. For example, people who like chocolate will find their taste buds going crazy when a double fudge nut brownie is brought to the table. There is nothing sinful about their physical reaction. God made us react that way to certain foods. Whether or not people are on a diet has nothing to do with how their taste buds react. The brownie serves as an external stimuli that causes an internal reaction. If the brownie is outside the parameters of what people believe God would have them eat at that time, the brownie becomes a temptation. No sin has taken place, however, until a bite is taken.

The same is true for sexual temptation, the temptation to lie, the temptation to gossip, and even the temptation to be lazy. All of these temptations begin with a thought that carries with it some sort of emotional punch. Sometimes it is so strong we are overwhelmed with condemnation. But the thought of doing something evil, even when combined with the desire to do it, is not a sin, only a temptation.

There is another reason we know that being tempted could not possibly be a sin. Jesus was tempted. The writer of Hebrews tells us,

> For we do not have a high priest who cannot sympathize with our weaknesses, but One who has been tempted in all things as we are, yet without sin.
>
> —Hebrews 4:15

This verse makes two important points. First of all, Jesus was tempted just like we are. If our temptation is a sin, so was His; our temptations are just like His. Second, Jesus never sinned. If Jesus was tempted and yet never sinned, then temptation cannot be a sin.

When Jesus was tempted on the mountain as described in Matthew 4, Satan put ideas in His head much like he does ours. One of these ideas certainly conjured up some strong feelings and emotions in our Lord:

> Then Jesus was led up by the Spirit into the wilderness to be tempted by the devil. And after He had fasted forty days and forty nights, He then became hungry. And the tempter came and said to Him, "If you are the Son of God, command that these stones become bread."
>
> —Matthew 4:1–3

This passage makes it clear that Jesus had sinful ideas bombarding His mind and that He had feelings right along with them. The text goes so far as to tell us that "He became hungry." Yet even with all of that, it was not considered sin, for He never ate.

We serve a just and righteous God. He will not hold us responsible for things over which we have no control. He knows Satan is working full time to flood our ears, eyes, and minds with things that will sidetrack us. God will not judge us for those evil thoughts that dart through our minds, not even for those longings and desires that often accompany certain thoughts. On the contrary, He sent His Son to enable us to successfully deal with the onslaught of temptation. Temptation is not a sin; it is simply Satan's attempt to make us fall.

2. Spiritually Mature People Are Not Harassed By Temptation.

I am always amazed at how people respond when I share something I am struggling with in my personal life. Whether it is from the pulpit or in private, their response is usually the same. "I can't imagine *you* being tempted like that!" Behind their amazement stands another misunderstanding concerning temptation: *spiritually mature people are not harassed by temptation*.

All of us will face temptation the rest of our lives. There is no escaping it. When people tell me they are struggling with temptation, I want to say, "So what's new?" Somewhere we have gotten the erroneous idea that our ultimate goal as Christians is to come to a place in our lives where we are never tempted. Ironically, the very opposite is true. The more godly we become, the more of a threat we become to Satan. Thus, the harder he works to bring us down.

Temptation will always be a part of the believer's life. Maturity only causes Satan to increase the pressure. So if you feel the pressure is on like never before, praise the Lord!! That could be an indication that Satan sees you as a threat to his work in this world. Don't be discouraged. In the words of James, "Consider it all joy, my brethren, when you encounter various trials" (James 1:2).

I have heard people say, "If you are truly filled with the Holy Spirit, you will be above temptation." That is not only unbiblical; it is antibiblical. The Bible teaches just the opposite. Jesus was certainly filled with the Holy Spirit. Yet not even He escaped temptation.

This particular misunderstanding is the reason many people fail to pray on a regular basis for their spiritual leaders. They falsely assume that these spiritual giants have no problems, much less any serious temptation. Your spiritual leaders need your prayers more than anybody else. Satan is probably working overtime to bring them down. He knows that when godly men and women fall, seeds of doubt are planted in the minds of all those who held them in esteem. What's worse, it confirms to the lost world what they already suspected: "The church is full of hypocrites and liars; there's nothing to religion." Pray for your pastor and church leaders! They struggle with the same temptations you do. Nobody is immune.

As long as you are on this earth in its present condition, you will be faced with temptation. The more "spiritual" you become, the more of a target you become. As your spiritual maturity and responsibility increase, so must your sensitivity to and dependence on the Holy Spirit. If the Son of God never reached a point where He was above being tempted, it is highly unlikely you would ever reach such a point in this lifetime, either.

3. Once a Sin or Habit Is Truly Dealt With, Temptation in That Particular Area Will Subside.

This misunderstanding really leaves people confused and discouraged. Once again, it is because their expectations are unrealistic. Often Christians will struggle with a particular sin for a long time—sometimes for years. Then something will happen, and they will be delivered. Usually deliverance comes through a new understanding of their power in Christ over sin.

For a while they will walk in such victory that they will get lulled into thinking that they are above falling back into that particular sin and that they are beyond being tempted by it. Sooner or later, however, a situation will arise, and they will be tempted once again. Many times the fact that they are even "temptable" sends them into such a tail-spin that they crash. This one failure may be so discouraging that it catapults them right back into the very sin from which they had been delivered.

This is exactly what happened to a friend of mine who had been delivered from an addiction to pornography. He went for months without even being tempted. He thought the problem was behind him once and for all and then WHAM! He found himself feeling the same way he used to feel and thinking about things he had not thought about for months. The very fact that he could feel that way again almost overwhelmed him. As he tells the story, it was like Satan was whispering in his ear, "Nothing has changed; you are still the same person as before. Why kid yourself? If you had really changed, you wouldn't feel this way or want to do these things." He made the mistake of falling for Satan's lie and gave in to the temptation.

This one incident made such a deep impression that he almost gave up the fight completely. He explained to me how he became very introspective, always looking for some hidden problem that caused his downfall. Through all this searching, he realized what had happened. He admitted that as the weeks and months passed after his deliverance, he had grown lazy in his Bible study and prayer time. He had stopped renewing his mind, and he took pride in the new truths God had revealed to him. He admitted that he really believed he was above being tempted with pornography again.

Today he walks in victory once more. Not because of a

one-time event, but because he has come to grips with his own frailty. He knows now that temptation can come at any time and that he must walk in moment by moment dependency upon Christ. If you were to ask him whether or not he has been delivered from his addiction to pornography, he would tell you, "I am being delivered daily." By that he means every day he has the potential to be tempted; but every day God is giving him the victory. I have watched this fellow develop into one of the most godly young men I know. Yet he will never reach the point of being beyond temptation.

God has promised to deliver you from giving in to temptation. Nowhere has He promised to deliver you from *being tempted*. Satan knows your weak points. If he has tripped you up in an area before, you can rest assured he will come at you again from the same angle. He is smart. He knows when to back off for a time. He also knows when your pride has set you up to fall.

When you are tempted time and time again with the same temptation, don't automatically assume that you have some deep, underlying problem. Neither should you assume that you are any more "sinful" than anybody else. Nowhere in Scripture is a person's spirituality judged on the basis of frequency of temptation. Satan propagates this misunderstanding so that you and I will become discouraged and give in to temptation. The truth is that we are all weaker in some areas than in others. Satan will always capitalize on our weaknesses. Therefore, we will experience recurring temptations for the rest of our lives.

4. We Fall into Temptation.

It is not uncommon for someone to say, "You know, I was going along just great when all of a sudden I *fell* into temptation." The notion that people *fall* into temptation points to another misunderstanding. People do not *fall* into temptation. Such phraseology portrays sinners as victims, innocent bystanders who are swept into sin against their will. That is not the case at all.

Someone may object, "But you don't know the pressure I was under. It was unbearable. I couldn't help what happened." That objection is simply an attempt to bypass personal responsibility for sin. It is an attempt to put the blame somewhere else. We do not fall into temptation; we *choose* to sin. In every single temptation there is a point at which we cast a deciding ballot either to sin or not to sin. No one can cast it for us—regardless of the pressure we may be facing.

It is true that we do not choose to be tempted. In that respect it could be said that we fall prey to temptation. But being surprised by temptation is never a cause or an excuse to sin. Temptation in no way impairs our freedom to choose. And as long as we have that freedom, we are always responsible for our actions.

When someone falls into a hole or falls off a bicycle, it is usually not the result of a conscious decision to do so. On the contrary, something overtakes the individual and forces him down against his will. Giving in to temptation is different. Sin, in the context of a temptation, is always the result of a decision.

Regardless of the pressure, we still hold the deciding vote. Never are we forced, kicking and screaming against our will, to give in to temptation. Temptation is not something we *fall* into; it is something we choose to *give* in to. That is why Christ is just in judging men and punishing according to the deeds. If sin was something we fell into, then Christ would have no right to hold us personally accountable.

I've never heard anyone say, "I don't know what came over me. I just found myself doing good things. I couldn't help it. I didn't really want to do all those nice things; I just fell into it." We always take personal responsibility for the good things we do, don't we? It is only the bad we want to pass off as unavoidable. But we are responsible for both. Just as we *choose* to do good, so we *choose* to do evil.

5. God Is Disappointed and Displeased When We Are Tempted.

When we are tempted, the feelings of condemnation are often so strong that we are sure God must be disappointed; He must be shaking His head in disgust. Surely He finds it hard to believe that we would even entertain such ideas after all He has done for us.

In one respect we have already dealt with this misunderstanding. Since temptation is not a sin and even the most spiritual people are tempted, God could not possibly be disappointed or displeased when we are tempted. Certainly He was not disappointed in His own Son when He was tempted!

We continue to feel we have disappointed God when we are tempted because there is a tendency to confuse how we feel about ourselves with how God feels about us. When we feel disappointed in ourselves, we assume God is disappointed as well. Such, however, is not always the case. As we have seen, much of the disappointment we feel toward ourselves in regard to temptation has to do with failing to live up to unrealistic expectations to begin with. As long as we have unrealistic expectations, we will disappoint ourselves.

God, on the other hand, has no expectations. He is omniscient; He already knows about every temptation that will come our way as well as how we will respond. Nothing takes Him by surprise; therefore, He does not even have the potential to be disappointed.

There is another reason we know God is not disappointed when we are tempted. Temptation is one of His primary tools to develop character and faith in believers. James made this clear when he wrote,

Consider it all joy, my brethren, when you encounter various trials, knowing that the testing of your faith produces endurance. And let endurance have its perfect result, that you may be perfect and complete, lacking in nothing.

—James 1:2–4

When we are tempted, our faith and character are tested. When we resist successfully, we come out stronger.

If you have ever seen a dog trained, you have seen this principle in action. The trainer at some point in the training process will tell the dog to stay and then put something the dog loves to eat just a few feet away. A well-trained dog will wait until permission is granted before going over to the food. Setting the food before the dog tests the animal's loyalty to his trainer. In the same way, temptation tests our love for Christ. For this reason, James said,

Blessed is a man who perseveres under trial; for once he has been approved, he will receive the crown of life, which the Lord has promised to those who love Him.

—James 1:12

God could not possibly be disappointed when we are tempted. James said that God rewards those who are tempted—if they persevere. It is not temptation itself that grieves God; He is displeased when we give in to temptation.

God is not disappointed when you are tempted. He has no reason to be. He knows Satan is out to get you. Remember, God gave you the foundational desires Satan capitalizes upon when you are tempted. He also gave you the power to choose. There is a sense in which God gave you the potential to be tempted in the first place. He is not disappointed.

6. Temptation Is Overcome By Running.

Earlier I said that one method of defending ourselves against temptation was to avoid situations that set us up to be tempted. That is, we should flee temptation whenever possible. Now it is true that fleeing certain places and relationships does facilitate our victory at times. However, running doesn't solve the problem of temptation in general. Temptation is not a war waged at a particular geographical location. The battlefield of temptation is the mind. Thus, running does not always guarantee victory nor does it do away with temptation.

I meet people all the time who are changing jobs, churches, and even cities in order to "escape" temptation. Most of the time they end up in a situation just like the one they left. Why? They changed their circumstances but they never changed themselves. They failed to renew their minds, thus allowing God to change their character and heart.

What's going on internally ultimately determines what happens externally. God wants to change your heart. He wants you to grow so that you can stand firm in the midst of temptation. He isn't going to take you out of the world. He has left you here to have an impact on it. That means you are going to face temptation. Spending all your time trying to avoid temptation will ultimately bring you to a point where you will be too isolated from society to have any impact. There is a time to run and a time to stand.

Cutting Through the Confusion

God does not want us to be ignorant about temptation. He wants us to know the truth. Part of Satan's scheme is to confuse the facts concerning this issue of temptation. In this chapter we have examined six commonly held theories regarding temptation. None of them could be supported biblically. In every case the Bible teaches just the opposite. If you have held to one or more of these misunderstandings, you need to begin today to renew your mind to the truth: being tempted is not a sin; spiritual people are tempted, too; victory now does not guarantee victory later; we do not fall into temptation—we choose to sin; God is not disappointed when we are tempted; running is not always the best way to overcome temptation.

At first you may find it difficult to put away these misunderstandings. You may have held to some of these for years. But until you begin to see your temptations the way God sees them, you will feel a weight of responsibility God never intended for you to feel; your expectation level will remain totally unrealistic. Consequently, you will become discouraged and unmotivated. God wants you to be free, and freedom comes through knowing the truth. Now that you have seen the truth, work to make it a part of your experience.

CHAPTER 13

Why We Continue to Fall

NOTHING IS MORE frustrating for a counselor than a counselee who appears to be doing everything he or she is told and yet comes back week after week to report, "It didn't work." Having exhausted all the usually effective methods, the counselor will either admit failure or do some further probing into the nature of the counselee's problem. Because this is a book rather than a series of counseling sessions, it is doubtful that you have had time to apply all of the principles outlined in the preceding chapters. For those who have, and yet still continue to fall, here are three suggestions as to why nothing has worked so far. These are a culmination of things I have discovered in my counseling with others as well as in my own passage through the mine field of temptation.

Who, Me?

One reason we continue to fall is that *we deny that we have a problem*. We know we have some things we need to work on. But a "problem"? No way. That sounds too serious. Consequently, we don't pursue a solution with the determination we need to see it through to the end. By suppressing the truth about our situation, we automatically cut ourselves off from getting the help we need.

The real danger is that people tend to ignore the truth

until what began as a small thing becomes a major problem. This pattern of behavior is common among alcoholics and drug abusers. Instead of approaching their problem as a full-blown addiction problem, they treat it like it's simply a matter of balance. "I just need to cut back."

Going to the doctor is about my least favorite thing to do. When I start feeling under the weather, my tendency is to say, "This is just a head cold. A couple of aspirin and I'll be fine." Regardless of how I'm really feeling, I convince myself that I'm not really *sick*; I'm just reacting to the change in the weather. If in fact I do have a virus of some kind, treating it like a head cold or the result of changing atmospheric conditions will be worthless. I will continue to be sick until I get an accurate diagnosis of my problem and then follow the prescribed treatment.

The same is true when it comes to dealing with sin. Most of us underestimate the power of sin and overestimate our spirituality. As long as you treat a bona fide problem like it is just part of your personality or the result of pressure at work or anything else besides what it is, you will find no relief. You must face your failure head-on to get serious enough to do anything about it. Perhaps you continue to fall to the same temptation because you have not admitted to yourself that you have a genuine problem.

I Surrender All

Another reason we may continue to fall is that *we have not surrendered to the lordship of Christ*. By that I mean we have not recognized Christ's unconditional right to rule and reign over every area of our lives. As long as we refuse to give up our right to rule in a particular area of our lives, we will never know victory.

Oftentimes we play a power game with God. We want Him to give us the power we need to have victory in our lives. But we aren't willing to surrender that area to His unchallenged rule. We want to use His power for our ends.

I talked to one of our singles recently who wanted me to explain how to deal with peer pressure. His problem was that whenever he spent time with his old college buddies, he was tempted to do the things they all used to do together in college. Over and over he had given in to the temptation to do these things.

I began to explain to him the wisdom principle outlined in chapter 8. I told him that part of God's answer may be for him to find some new friends. As soon as I mentioned that prospect, his body language told me he didn't think that was a good idea at all. "But they are my best friends," he argued. "We've been best friends for years!"

I explained to him that his real problem wasn't the things he had mentioned earlier that were normally associated with his friends. His real problem was lordship. He wasn't willing to allow Jesus Christ to be Lord of all his relationships. I asked him if he was willing to surrender all his relationships to the lordship of Christ, even if it meant breaking off some relationships completely. He was not ready to do that.

His response is characteristic of how we all respond at times to this issue of lordship. We want our lives to go "right." But we want them to go right on *our* terms, by *our* standards. We want God's help, but not to the point that it interferes with our plans and desires.

God is not interested in giving us victory for victory's sake or victory for the sake of making life easier for us. Power over sin is the means by which we are freed to serve Christ more effectively. It is not something God hands out to make life smoother for us.

The Missing Father

A father in our fellowship came to see me about his fourteen-year-old son. He said that they did not communicate anymore and that Jimmy did not respond to authority like he used to. As we continued to talk, it became clear that part of the problem had to do with this man's work schedule. He left early in the morning, before his son was up. And he returned late at night, usually after his son was in bed. On Sunday it wasn't unusual for him to go into the office after church and stay there until early evening. In his profession he could basically set his own hours, but he had convinced himself that the long hours were necessary to provide adequately for his family.

I explained to this man the relationship between his being away from home so much and his son's loss of interest and respect. I made it clear that part of the answer would be for him to change his schedule. Our conversation came to an abrupt halt. You see, he may have been interested in restoring his relationship with his son, but he was interested in doing it on his terms, not God's. He wanted things to be "right," but he was not willing to surrender his work schedule to the lordship of Christ.

The real issue when it comes to lordship is trust. We hold back areas of control because we don't trust God to do it "right." We think He will let a need go unmet. Or that He won't meet it the way we think is best. We are afraid God will wait too long to do something. We just don't trust Him, so we hold back.

It is ironic that we want Him to come rushing into our lives when things get out of our control, when there is a death or an emergency. At those times we are more than willing to admit our inadequacy and our dependence on Him. But as soon as things return to normal, as soon as life gets "easy" again, we are afraid to hand it all over to Him. Think about it. If God can be trusted when we are most vulnerable and helpless, can He not be trusted in the times when things are going smoothly?

God wants control over every area of your life. Not partial control, total control. He wants you to be victorious over temptation. But He wants you to be victorious for His purposes, not yours. You may not have achieved victory over temptation because you are holding to the reins of your life and trying to get God to intervene in the rough spots. That isn't the way God works. He wants all of you. And when He knows you are His, He will do whatever He needs to do to make you into an effective servant for His kingdom.

"Forgetting What Lies Behind"

There is a third reason for our repeated failures. *We continually focus on past failure.* To focus on the past causes us to be problem oriented. We allow our past failures to persuade us that we will never change, that there is no use even trying to do things differently. When we are tempted, we are set up to fall. Mentally, we have already been defeated.

The truth is that God has made available to you the power to change. The sins of the past need not characterize your life in the future. No one is destined to be a certain way throughout a lifetime. Your past sins should simply serve as a reminder of God's grace and forgiveness. But even then, they should not be the focus of your attention.

There is another problem with focusing on our past failures, however. It is easy to allow our past failures to serve as an excuse to sin again. "Well," we reason, "I have already done it once. I might as well do it again." We are easily deceived into thinking that "one more time" will not really hurt anything. The tragedy is that each "one more time" just keeps the sin cycle alive in our lives. A habit is simply a string of individual sins committed on separate occasions.

To commit a sin one more time does matter because each time we sin, it just ingrains that habit a little bit deeper into our emotional being. Sin becomes more and more entrenched. Each time we give in, it becomes that much more difficult to say no the next time.

These are the hazards of focusing on our past failures. We get bogged down or deceived. The apostle Paul certainly had some things in his past that could have slowed him down. However, in reference to his past he wrote,

Brethren, I do not regard myself as having laid hold of it yet; but one thing I do: *forgetting what lies behind* and reaching forward to what lies ahead, I press on toward the goal for the prize of the upward call of God in Christ Jesus.

—Philippians 3:13–14, emphasis added

Paul understood that a believer must put the past behind and move on. Do you have a tendency to focus on the past? Do you rehearse the sins of your past over and over in your mind? Does reflection on your past sins cause you to doubt that things will ever change? If that is the case, then join with the apostle Paul by turning your focus toward the future, toward the things you want to see God do in your life. The past is something you can do nothing about. The future, however, is whatever you allow God to make it.

Could It Be?

Think for just a moment. Could it be that you have a genuine *problem* with sin but are unwilling to deal with it as such? Is Jesus Christ Lord of every known area in your life? Is He Lord of your family, friends, jobs, goals, relationships, time, money? Is there an area you are holding back? Do you have a tendency to focus on the past? Do you use your past failures as an excuse to sin? Are you overwhelmed with such a deep sense of failure that you find no reason to try anymore?

If you answered yes to any of these questions, then you may have just discovered why you continue to fall. As long as you refuse to surrender fully to the lordship of Christ, His power will be cut off. As long as you treat a problem as anything but a problem, it will never go away. And as long as you focus on the past, you will never find strength to move ahead. Ask God to give you insight into how you can correct your attitude.

CHAPTER 14

After We Fail, What Then?

YOU HAVE BEEN reading an entire book dedicated to helping you overcome temptation, but you went out and blew it anyway. Now what? Do you give up? Do you reconcile yourself to a life of defeat? Do you take the book back for a refund? What do you do?

In this final chapter I want to outline what I call the steps to recovery. These seven steps or stages are necessary if you are to emerge from failure victorious rather than defeated. The idea of coming out of failure victoriously may sound like a contradiction in terms. But God has provided a way by which even your worst failure can be transformed into great gain. And not only for you, but for as many people as you are willing to share it with.

It is important for us to respond properly to failure. Oftentimes our incorrect response to failure sets us up to fall again. The more we fail, the more discouraged we get and the less faith we have in God's ability to make us victorious. In the book of Psalms David records his prayer of remorse after sinning with Bathsheba. This prayer includes the seven steps that I believe are necessary for all of us to follow after we have given in to temptation. Once we complete these steps, we actually emerge from our failure stronger than before. We will be more suitable for God's service, and we will be better prepared for the next time we are tempted.

God has a beautiful way of taking what is negative and turning it around for His glory—if we let Him. Think about it. The greatest tragedy in all of history—the death of the Son of God—turned out to be mankind's greatest blessing—the resurrection of the Son of God. If we will respond properly to our failure, God can use it to bring Himself glory and to better prepare us for His service.

Repent!

The first stage in the recovery process is *repentance*. Two counterfeit forms of repentance are often passed off as the real thing. One of them goes like this, "Lord, I am really sorry I got caught." The other sounds like this, "Lord, I am really sorry I sinned. I certainly hope I can do better next time." Both of these are prompted out of guilt or embarrassment, not a heartfelt sense of remorse over the fact that almighty God has been grieved. People who pray such prayers have no intention of changing. They are simply attempting to get God off their backs.

Genuine repentance involves several things. First of all, confession. Not just, "Lord, I am sorry for my mistake," but, "Lord, I have sinned against You." Confession acknowledges guilt. Second, repentance involves the recognition that the sin was against God. Notice what David said,

> Against Thee, Thee only, I have sinned,
> And done what is evil in Thy sight.
> —Psalm 51:4

Now that does not mean he failed to recognize that he had sinned against Bathsheba and her husband. He was saying that he realized that his sin was primarily against God. Against the backdrop of all the grace and goodness God had showered down upon him, David's sin was primarily against God.

All of us need to recognize that our sin is primarily against God. Other people may be hurt as well, but when we hold our sin up to the unconditional love and grace of God as expressed through the giving of His Son, we see clearly that there is where sin looks its darkest. We see sin for what it is, the most extreme expression of ingratitude. So repentance includes a confession of our guilt, recognition that our sin is against God, and two other things.

Repentance includes taking full responsibility for our sin. David clearly accepted full responsibility for his actions with Bathsheba. He said,

> Wash *me* thoroughly from *my* iniquity,
> And cleanse *me* from *my* sin.
> For I know *my* transgressions,
> And *my* sin is ever before *me*.
>   —Psalm 51:2–3, emphasis added

Nowhere do we find him saying, "Now, Lord, You know it takes two. I wasn't the only one involved. She should have been more careful than to bathe right underneath my balcony. You know I am only human." David never accused Bathsheba. He never mentioned her name.

Whenever we catch ourselves blaming someone else for our sin, our repentance is incomplete. If we are truly repentant, we will take full responsibility for sin, no matter what happened or who was involved. Regardless of the nature of the temptation, ultimately we are the ones who make the decision to give in.

Last, repentance requires total honesty with God. Repentance is not complete without honesty. Think about this for a moment. Which of the following two qualities are more important when it comes to our fellowship and relationship with God, *honesty* or *holiness*? You know, we won't always be holy, but we can always be honest. I believe God is looking for us to be honest about our sin—honest about our weaknesses, our failures, and our frustrations. Honesty promotes fellowship. As long as we continue to be open and honest with God, He can continue to work with us, even after we have committed our most grievous sin.

We get into trouble when we start trying to cover things up. "Now, Lord, I know I have made a mistake. But after all, everybody makes mistakes. Nobody's perfect." Responding like that is simply avoiding the real issue and is therefore dishonest. As long as we approach God in that fashion, there is not much He can do with us.

What Happens Then?

Before we go to the second stage in the recovery process, I want to say something about God's discipline in connection with repentance. The Bible teaches that God disciplines those who are disobedient. The Scripture is full of illustrations of God's discipline. The story of David and Bathsheba is one of the best examples. I believe, however, that when true repentance follows quickly on the heels of sin, the discipline is lessened.

When David committed adultery with Bathsheba, he did not repent immediately. It was some time later when David finally faced up to what he had done. And even then he did not do it of his own accord. God had to send a prophet to confront him (2 Sam. 12). It was only after Nathan told him the story of the man who had the many sheep stealing from the man who had one that David realized the great evil he had done. That was when David repented of his sin. The discipline that followed, however, was very severe in nature, and part of the reason for the severity was David's failure to repent sooner.

It is my personal conviction that if you and I deal with our sin genuinely, openly, and immediately, God will lessen the severity of our discipline. This makes sense in light of the nature of discipline anyway. Discipline is for the purpose of getting us to change, to obey. If God sees that we want to cooperate and that we have purposed in our hearts to obey the next time around, there is no need for discipline, except as a reminder.

When we let our sin go on and on with no intention of stopping until we are finally caught, it is too late to escape the disciplining hand of God. For our own sake, and for the testimony of His kingdom's sake, He cannot let us continue in our sin. The longer we put off repentance in our lives, the greater our discipline will be. Those who are wise will repent quickly.

Accept God's Forgiveness

The second stage in the recovery process is *acceptance of God's forgiveness*. Oftentimes this is difficult because we feel so guilty, especially if it is a sin we have repeatedly committed. Sometimes we just feel plain stupid coming to God with it again, but that is what we must do.

Remember, when Jesus died on the cross two thousand years ago for your sin, He died for all your sins—past, present, and future. Your sin causes you embarrassment because you expect better of yourself. But God doesn't. He already knew about it. Even as you prayed time before last and promised Him you would never do it again, He already knew you would. And He had already made provision for it. So you need not be embarrassed; you need not avoid Him.

Someone always makes the comment at this point, "Well, if all our sin is paid for, past, present, and future, why do we have to repent and confess every time?" For the simple reason that until we face up to what we have done, we are out of fellowship with the Father. What if I steal something that belongs to you and you know about it? You can forgive me in your heart and never think about it again. But when I know that you know, I can never act natural or feel at ease around you until I confess what I have done.

The same is true in our relationship with God. Until we confess our sins—one at a time—we remain out of fellowship with Him. The guilt will remain as far as we are concerned, and we will never experience the peace we are intended to have. We will continue to avoid Him, and we will be set up to fall again. That is why it is so important to keep short accounts with God. Satan would have us avoid confession and repentance as long as possible. That way we are prone to sin because we are running from God. And you remember where that got Jonah, don't you?

Along with accepting God's forgiveness, we must forgive ourselves. We shouldn't make the mistake of holding ourselves more accountable than the God who created us does. If He says our sin is paid for, then it is paid for. We can't try to make it up to Him through good works. That is impossible. If the One we sinned against no longer holds our sin against us what right do we have to do so? In essence we are usurping His authority. We must just accept it by faith and move on. As long as we feel we must punish ourselves or in some way make it up to Him, we will avoid Him. And just like the people who refuse to accept His forgiveness, we will play right into the hands of Satan.

Don't mistake God's discipline as evidence that He has not forgiven you. If He had not forgiven you, He would not be disciplining you; He would have to punish you. When people are punished, they are "paid back" for what they have done. The Bible says that the punishment for any sin is death (Rom. 6:23). If God were going to punish you for your sin, He would have to put you to death physically and then send you to hell eternally. The fact that God is only disciplining you is evidence that you are one of His children and therefore forgiven! (For a more in-depth discussion on the subject, see chapter 9, "Forgiving Ourselves," in *Forgiveness*.)

Restitution

The third stage in the recovery process involves *restitution*. You must make restitution to those against whom you have sinned. Sometimes this is not always easy. If you have stolen something, you can give that back without much trouble—and pay for any damages as well. But how do you make restitution when you have robbed someone of purity or honor or reputation?

You must ask that person to forgive you. By that, I do not mean you simply say that you are sorry. You must ask for forgiveness. Make it clear that you realize you have sinned against the person and God and that you are willing to do whatever is possible to remedy the situation.

In making restitution, you need to be careful not to involve other people. You are not called on to repent of anyone else's sin, just your own. In the same way, you need to make sure you are confessing your sin to the person you sinned against. You may be tempted to confess your sin to someone who has nothing to do with your sin. This is usually a ploy to relieve yourself of the guilt you are bearing. This is a waste of time and it can be harmful. Anytime you involve a third party, you run the risk of others finding out as well, which could result in embarrassment to you and the one to whom you really owe the apology. The one exception is when you share your burden with an accountability partner beforehand. But even then, there is no need to go into detail about the sin. As a general rule, it is best not to involve someone else.

Accept God's Discipline

The next stage in the recovery process is *acceptance of God's discipline*. Oftentimes we do not recognize the disciplining hand of God. When there are personal consequences resulting from our sin, such as an injury or a financial loss, we can usually recognize those right away. But sometimes God's discipline comes in forms that at first seem to have no relationship to what we have done. In time, however, the truth usually becomes apparent.

When we recognize that we are being disciplined, one indisputable sign that we really mean business for God is that we don't fight it. By willingly accepting His discipline, we are acknowledging our guilt and His sovereign right to exercise authority over us.

When people resist the discipline of God, it is evidence that they have yet to come to grips with their sin and with the nature of sin itself. By resisting God's discipline, they are saying, "I don't deserve this. I deserve better. What I did wasn't really so bad." Their understanding of sin and what it cost God is so deficient that it is unlikely they will do much to guard against repeating the same error again and again.

On the other hand, people who accept the discipline of God realize that His discipline is for their own protection. They do not view it as something negative. They see it as an expression of His love, for that is exactly what it is.

Imagine for a moment a child who has been told repeatedly not to play in the street. But he goes right ahead and does it anyway. His parents, if they are wise, will discipline him. Why? Because they are the parents and he is just a child and how dare he break their rules? No. They know that if he doesn't learn to stay out of the street, he could be killed or crippled. The disciplinary action they choose may seem painful to their child, but a simple spanking is far better than being hit by a car. A lesser evil is used to guard the child from a much greater evil.

So it is when God disciplines us. He is trying to keep us from the greater harm that comes from involvement with sin. We will not fully appreciate the love God has expressed toward us through His discipline until we get to heaven.

Live and Learn

The fifth stage in the recovery process involves *identification of the lesson or lessons* God is attempting to teach us through our failure. The tragedy of skipping this stage is that the whole series of events becomes a waste of time. God is in the process of bringing something good out of the mess we have caused. However, if we don't discover what He is trying to teach us, the whole process is short-circuited.

When it comes to learning from our mistakes, we need to keep in mind humility, purity, and instruction. When we fall, we should pray, "Lord, humble my spirit before You. Purify my sinful heart. And instruct me in Your ways so that this habit can be broken and I can experience the freedom You have made available."

Since pride is always connected with our sin, we should take every available opportunity to allow God to rid our lives of it. The same is true of impurity, whether it is moral impurity or impure motives. These are two areas we always need work in. Each time we are working back through the stages of recovery, God breaks us little by little of our pride and impurity.

Let me ask you a question. When you blow it, do you ask God to teach you something? Or do you rush through a quick 1 John 1:9 type of prayer and keep moving? The truth is that you should always take the time to learn something from your mistakes. Otherwise you are bound to keep repeating them. Not only that, you rob somebody else of the privilege of learning from your mistakes.

When your attitude is right, you are going to want to learn everything you can. Your first response won't be, "God, get the pressure off. Relieve me of my guilt. Make me feel better. AMEN." I know you don't use those words, but does that reflect your attitude sometimes when you are approaching God after you have sinned? If it does, you are not really serious about making any real changes in your life.

You do not desire an intimate relationship with God. You basically want to be left alone to do your own thing without any outside interference.

God wants to teach us something through our failures. But as is the case in all of God's lessons, only those who are paying attention are going to learn them. Only those who are seeking Him will find Him. Only those with ears to hear will hear Him. Those who fail and learn nothing have wasted not only an opportunity to learn but have pretty much guaranteed for themselves another trip through the recovery process.

Get Help!

The sixth stage in the recovery process involves *consultation with a qualified counselor.* If you continue to struggle with the same temptation and nothing seems to help, you may need professional help. By professional, I mean someone who can listen and help you gain insight into why you are struggling the way you are. We discussed in chapter 4 the fact that sometimes there are root causes of the temptations we face. You may need help discovering the root of your particular problem. It could be something related to your childhood that you cannot remember. It may be something more recent that you have failed to connect with your present temptations. Whatever it is, you may need a counselor to help you make the discovery that could set you free.

If you are too proud to ask for help, you will be the loser. I have talked to counselors more times than I can remember. All of us run into things in our lives that just don't make any sense. Sometimes one basic insight can unlock doors that have kept us prisoners for years, but it takes someone trained to know how to get to those remote places in our memories and experiences.

Don't ever be too proud to say, "Hey, I need help. I have run up against something that I don't quite know how to handle." All of us need the objective opinion and insight of someone else at some point. That is why God has equipped counselors and made them available to the body of Christ.

Teach Others

The last stage in the recovery process is *readiness to share what we have learned* with others. Consider what David said,

> Create in me a clean heart, O God,
> And renew a steadfast spirit within me.
> Do not cast me away from Thy presence.
> And do not take Thy Holy Spirit from me.
> Restore to me the joy of Thy salvation,
> And sustain me with a willing spirit.
> Then I will teach transgressors Thy ways,
> And sinners will be converted to Thee.
> —Psalm 51:10–13

David wanted God to completely cleanse his heart and restore his relationship. After that process was complete, David wanted God to allow him to teach other sinners the ways of God. And notice his goal: "And sinners will be converted to Thee." David wanted to take what he had learned and teach others.

When you and I have really repented of our sin, faced up to our responsibility and willingly accepted the consequences of what we have done, God will teach us some fabulous lessons. He will grant us deep insight into His Word. The process is not complete, however, until we make ourselves available to teach others what we have learned. By doing this, we demonstrate to God and to ourselves that we are totally given over to His purposes; we are His and His alone.

Don't misunderstand. By teaching others, I don't

necessarily mean in a formal sense, although it may come to that. Think of the blessings you have received from those who share their testimony of what God has done in their lives. Regardless of how God chooses to use you, you must be willing to share with others the lessons God has taught you. After all, that is half the reason He taught you to begin with.

When you hit bottom, who would you rather talk to? Somebody who always seems to be doing exceptionally well and appears untouched by sorrow and pain? Or somebody who like you has hit bottom, but is slowly making progress? We all need someone we can identify with. Through your failure and then your proper response to your failure, God is preparing you to be an instrument of encouragement in someone else's life.

Be Careful!

You should use discretion when you share the lessons God has taught you through your failures. Be wise. Don't tell the details of your sin. That is not really important. Avoid making sin sound glamorous. Hollywood does an excellent job of that. The filmmakers certainly don't need your help. Too much detail often stirs people's imagination and curiosity to the point of causing them to sin.

Focus on the lessons God has taught you. When you mention your sin, point out the consequences. Include the things that could have happened if God had not rescued you when He did. Oftentimes testimonies leave the impression that we can have our cake and eat it, too. That is, we can enjoy sin for a while, and then when we are good and ready, we can turn our lives over to the Lord. Testimonies should cause people to fear the consequences of sin so that they would never dream of becoming involved in similar sinful situations.

There is a second thing you need to keep in mind when you share with others what God has taught you.

Never say, "I have learned . . . ." No one has "learned" any-thing in the sense of reaching the point of no longer being subject to temptation in a given area. We are all still in the process of learning. A better way to say that is, "God is teaching me . . . ," or "Every day I continue to see . . . ."

As soon as you think you have finished learning something or even give that impression to someone, Satan is going to unleash a vicious attack. He loves to publicly em-barrass Christians. Mark it down. What you announce pub-licly, Satan will test you in privately.

We are all still learners. That is what a disciple is—a learner. We are all in the process of becoming what God wants us to be. No one has arrived. No one ever will in this lifetime. So when we share with others what God has taught us through our failures, we need to make sure we communi-cate it in such a way as to ensure a humble spirit on our part and realistic expectations on theirs.

Complete Recovery

God's plan for you includes several trips through the recovery process outlined in this chapter. We all fail. There is no question about that. The question you have to ask your-self is this: "Now that I have sinned, how will I respond?" You have two options. You can run from God and resist His discipline. Or you can genuinely repent of your sin, submit to His discipline, and learn everything you can in the pro-cess.

If you resist Him, you will be the loser. And so will all the people you could have helped if you had only allowed the Lord to teach you a few things. Nothing is sadder to me than believers who got stuck. God wanted to teach them something, and they decided they did not want to learn—so they stopped growing right there. They stagnated spiritually. Usually the issue was some sin they refused to repent of.

They ran from God, and now they are stuck. They refuse to let go of their sin, and God refuses to use them.

However, if you will work through these recovery stages, you will watch God take what started as a negative thing and transfer it into some of the most positive experiences of your life. At times it will be painful. But growth always is. The choice is yours. Not just once, but every time you give in to temptation. As you allow God to work you through this process, He will give you insight into why you are so susceptible to certain temptations. Your willingness to respond correctly to failure may provide you with the insight you need to be victorious next time.

Please don't waste your failures. Allow God to use them to mature you into the man or woman He wants you to be. Allow Him to turn your defeats into victories. Let Him take your failures and develop in you a testimony that will make an impact on all those who hear. The choice is yours. It is my prayer that everyone who reads this book will choose not to waste the failures, but will place them in the hands of the One who said,

Come to Me, all who are weary and heavy-laden, and I will give you rest. Take My yoke upon you, and learn from Me, for I am gentle and humble in heart; and you shall find rest for your souls. For My yoke is easy, and My load is light.

—Matthew 11:28–30

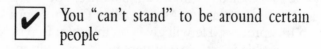
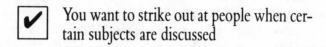
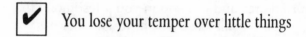
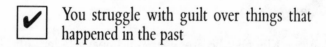
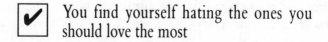